The Alcohol & Addiction Solution!

A breakthrough new approach to alcoholism and addictions using Neuro Restructuring Techniques!

Find the answers to how and why your mind sabotages your recovery… and what to do about it!

By William D. Horton, Psy. D.

© 2013 William D. Horton. All rights reserved.

Andrea J. Di Salvo, Editor

Copyright © 2013 by William D. Horton

All rights reserved. This book or any portion thereof may not be reproduced or used in any manner whatsoever without the express written permission of the publisher except for the use of brief quotations in a book review.

Printed in the United States of America

TABLE OF CONTENTS

Author's Note: Why Now?

As I get ready to write this book, I ponder the question, *why now?* After working in the recovery field for 30 years, I'm still amazed at the amount of misinformation and negativity there is about how people recover from addiction. I've given this much thought and contemplation, and have decided to share with you what I've found through working with thousands of clients and being active in my own personal recovery program.

I've been in a personal recovery program for 30 years and, unfortunately, the same problems that were present 30 years ago are present today. In fact, they're probably worse. This fact was brought to my awareness when I started going to more recovery meetings and watching people constantly relapse.

This became especially apparent as I was talking to a recovering alcoholic who, at one point, had several years of sobriety. Now, however, this person had not been able to go more than a few weeks clean and sober. This addict was doing what many people would call the "relapse shuffle." It seemed as if every week or two he was coming back into the A.A. program after a drinking relapse. As I talked to him, the person revealed that he was also seeing a therapist and seeking medical help, all to no avail. As we talked, my heart sank. I had been in that same boat, but had found a way out. I searched for ways to give this person the hope that he could—and should—recover. I shared with him some of the things we'll be talking about in this book, and gave him some steps to help get back on track.

Seeing others struggle this way not only breaks my heart, it also causes me to wonder, *why do some people make it and others don't?* I'm not the first to ask this question. This has been the great question that has plagued recovery professionals since the field started! Why do some people go to an A.A. or N.A. or O.A. meeting, go to therapy, go to a medical doctor or seek spiritual release, then kick their addiction and get on with their lives? Why are some able to do this, while others follow the same steps, but with much different results...never able to put down the drink or drug?

This led me back into some basic research and introspection into the recovery movement. I've had the honor of training many therapists in techniques to help their clients recover from alcoholism and other addictions. As I teach these classes, I find that the therapists who have worked with people and addictions all experience the same difficulties...clients who do well at the beginning, then hit some stressor and return to the addictive behavior. At the same time, I was delighted to learn that the people who *do*recover from this devastating, often fatal, illness seem to be able to not only physically, mentally and spiritually recover, but also seem to be able to reach into their brains to remove the need and the drive for the addiction. *This is the great secret of recovery.*

So, as I reached for answers, I was again drawn back into the basics of how people truly recover and get on with their lives. Here, I have to give credit to Dr. Ronald A. Ruden and his book, *The Craving Brain.* It was as I was in this process of searching for answers that I came across *The Craving Brain,* which gave medical and physical evidence for what I have seen and experienced in the last 30 years. The scientific research Ruden cited gave hard facts concerning a person's ability to physically reprogram his or her brain in order to recover from an addiction. It also propelled me onward in my quest for a better method to recover from alcoholism and other addictions. The object of this is to give hope to those who may have reached the point of hopelessness.

For over 25 years I ran a clinic that used hypnosis and Neuro Linguistic Programming to help people lose weight, stop smoking, lower stress, improve their sports games and, of course, overcome addictions. In treating over 20,000 clients, I've found ways to rapidly help my clients reprogram their minds. Now I've taken what works from psychotherapy, Alcoholics Anonymous, the medical community, and the best of the current alternative therapies. I've woven them into a new, unique way to, not just recover, but to become the person you always wanted to be.

This led me to develop the Apex of Alcohol and Addiction Recovery Program to walk people through the steps of recovery. I'll talk more about the program later. Hopefully, you'll realize as you are reading this that you deserve to invest in yourself and obtain what's needed for you to finally put your addiction problem behind you.

I've written this book in easy-to-understand words and terms because my goal is to help people recover, not to impress the professional community. The important thing is for you to get a hold of these ideas so you can develop your own unique recovery program.

So, back to the question, *why now*? The answer is: I want to bring hope to the hopeless and a way out to those that see no way out. I want to help the family members of those same people. The techniques and ideas that I share with you here not only saved my life, but gave me a life worth living. That's what I want for you.

This book is not intended to replace traditional therapy, A.A., medical treatment or spiritual advice. It *is* intended to help you recover from your addiction. The information in this book, and on the Apex Program, can be used by itself in the privacy of your home or with other treatment modalities under the care of a professional.

So, let's get started!

My Story: Thirty Years in the Field

I didn't get in trouble every time I drank, but every time I got in trouble, I was drinking.

It wasn't how much I drank; it's what the drink did to me.

It felt like I had a hole in my soul.

I had a hollowness in my heart.

I felt empty on the inside years before I ever took that first drink.

Those are some of the statements that I use to describe my drinking. It's been said that only an alcoholic can remember his first drink in vivid detail. That's certainly true for me.

I took my first drink when I was 14 years old. I was on the football team at the time, and I got the chance to drink with the cool, older guys on the team.

I'd always been outgoing, funny and engaging with other people. At the same time, I always felt, deep on the inside, that if people really knew me, they wouldn't like me. I felt empty. More than anything, I wanted to be a part of a group and to fit in. Looking back on it now, I can see that I was part of many groups, and that I did fit in. At the time, though, all I felt was empty and alone.

After I made the freshman football team, instead of feeling joy and happiness, I felt they must have let me in for some reason other than my skill…maybe pity. Then, after a game, the older guys went into the woods to party. Someone brought baby food jars full of cherry vodka. They passed the jars around and took sips. When my turn came, I drank the whole thing.

To this day, even 38 years later, even after 25 years completely sober, I can remember the drink burning as it went down. It hit my stomach and I felt it explode. It rippled through my body and gave me the sensation, for the first time in my life, that I was normal. I felt like I fit in. I felt good. I would chase that feeling for the next 15 self-destructive years.

By the time I was 16, I was drinking regularly and alcoholically. I was having blackouts. I was getting drunk when I really didn't want to. It was the only way I knew how to have fun, and I thought it made me cool. I even remember taking my boss downtown to get wine. As soon as I could drive, I knew where to go to get beer and wine. By the summer before my senior year, I was drinking regularly in bars. Probably the only thing that kept me out of jail was that, in 1973, drinking was encouraged over getting high.

After high school, I applied for and received a scholarship to go to college and become a Marine Corps pilot. Drinking, however, would also ruin this. Predictably, I got drunk one weekend and got into trouble. A judge suggested—strongly—that I go into active duty military to, as he put it, "Straighten myself out."

I joined the Army with the goal of becoming a helicopter pilot. I went to basic training and then on to advanced training. I had my sights on flight school, and maybe even West Point. Again, drinking would take this away from me.

I got in trouble both on base and off. A once-promising military career was aborted.

After the Army, I decided I wanted to be an actor. I applied to and was accepted into the American Academy of Dramatic Arts, the Harvard of the acting world. This is especially interesting since, when I applied, I'd only seen one play and had never acted at all. But it's said that God takes care of drunks and fools. I fit both categories!

I went to acting school and once more found that drinking was the only thing that helped me *feel* like I fit in. Instead, it alienated me and got me into trouble. Again, drinking removed a hopeful future.

I won't go into detail over all the little things that happened. I continued drinking and it continued robbing me of my life. During these times, in both the Army and the theater, I tried many things to stop drinking. I read about people who drank too much because they had a vitamin deficiency, so I took extra vitamins. I still got drunk, but my urine was colorful, and it probably helped keep me healthy. Even while all this was going on, I still held some type of job, mainly so I could afford drinking. I worked out and stayed in shape. In retrospect, it's funny that I had discipline in some areas, but none in that, the most important area of my life.

Finally, I got sick and tired of being sick and tired. I reached out for help. I was led into a long-term V.A. treatment program that began my recovery. The program used some psychotherapy and a lot of 12-step meetings. For the first time in my life, I was forced to look at me, to realize *I* was the problem.

This type of treatment helped me to a certain point. I reduced my drinking from daily drinking to periodic binges. I still couldn't tell you why or when I would drink. I just would. The therapy and 12-step program gave me some insight but couldn't get me over the hump. That stage continued for a couple of years.

I was lucky enough—even blessed, if you will—to come across the ideas that began to give me the tools I really needed, not just to stop drinking, but to become the type of person who doesn't need or want to drink. Those techniques took the best from the 12-step programs and the best from therapy and combined them with cutting-edge processes that really began to reprogram my mind.

Once I learned those self-hypnosis and Neuro Linguistic Programming (NLP) techniques, I was able to reprogram my mind and find my biobalance once and for all. After I learned those tools, I was able to see that the people who recovered from alcoholism through 12-step programs or therapy, or who simply quit, all did the same types of things at a subconscious level. This is the great secret to true recovery! It explains why some people fail and other people make it. Those who make it, somehow, all learn these same, internal biobalancing techniques.

Having found the solution for myself, my passion in life now is helping other people on this path. This is why I made the Apex Program. Now let me help you.

For help contact Dr Will Horton 941-468-8551

Who Is an Alcoholic or Addict?

When we look at the issue of who is an addict, or at least seems to be one, we look for some sort of physical characteristic to which we can point. The truth of the matter is, though, alcoholics and addicts are not just Skid Row types or addicts in a drug house. Addicts are doctors, lawyers, teachers, construction workers, policeman, military personnel, housewives, teenagers, senior citizens...the list is as varied as humans themselves. Addicts are the boy next door and the girl down the street, as well as the homeless in the shelters. They live in mansions, they live in the suburbs, and they live on the streets; they live everywhere people are.

Addiction is a worldwide problem, but hits home when it starts affecting your health, finances and personal life. Much of the time I'll talk about the addiction to alcohol, because that's the addiction I struggled with personally, but alcohol is only one kind of addiction among many. Addictions are as varied as the people who suffer from them. They could be addictions to chemicals like nicotine or hard drugs. They could even be addictions to activities such as overeating or gambling or sex.

You may be surprised to find behaviors like overeating lumped together with substance abuse, which is what most people think of when they consider addictions. When people are addicted to behaviors, though, they can actually become addicted to the chemicals that are produced naturally by the body. Imagine the thrill of placing a winning bet on your favorite football team...then imagine not being able to function without having that feeling all the time.

When that happens, addicts become so obsessed with those activities that they start to suffer from the same problems as alcoholics or drug addicts.

In every case, though, the addiction follows at least three, if not all, of seven steps listed by the American Psychiatric Association within a 12-month period:

1. Tolerance (need for increased amounts of the substance to achieve the desired effect or markedly diminished effect with continued use of the same amount of substance).
2. Withdrawal symptoms or continued use of the substance to reduce or avoid withdrawal symptoms.
3. Substance frequently taken in greater amounts or over longer periods of time than intended.
4. Persistent desire or unsuccessful attempts to control or reduce substance use.
5. A great deal of time spent in activities related to obtaining the substance (e.g., driving long distances), using the substance (e.g., chain-smoking), or recovering from its effects.
6. Important social, occupational, or recreational activities reduced or stopped because of substance use.
7. Continued use of the substance despite awareness of persistent or recurrent psychological or physical problems caused or exacerbated by its use.

Because you're reading this, and so are already looking for help with your own addiction, you might recognize several of those steps in your own life.

I've also included some of the classic questions that are asked from a clinical standpoint to decide if a person is an alcoholic. The 20 questions from Alcoholics Anonymous are some of the easiest to understand. To make it even simpler, there are a couple of very simple, very basic questions to ask yourself.

Do you use even when you know those around you–family members, friends, or employers–would rather you not?

Have you ever used more than you intended, especially when you intended not to?

Has someone close to you ever asked you to stop using, or limit your use, but you continue anyway?

Have you ever had any legal, employment, or life difficulties related to your use?

If you answered yes to any one of these, you probably have a problem. If you answered yes to more than one, you definitely have a problem. As they say, if it walks like a duck and quacks like a duck, it's a duck.

I like to say that people seek help when they're driven by one of the four Ls: their *lawyer,* their *liver,* their *livelihood,* or their *lovers.* Most of us only seek help when there's pressure. The fact that people continue in their addictions when they and others know it's a problem is a sure sign that they have crossed that invisible line.

When it comes to knowing you have a problem, though, it is more important to simply look at the facts and do an honest self-appraisal, as only you can, to decide if you have an addiction. This is the first step.

Since you have this book, and the Apex Program, let's proceed under the assumption that you're ready to accept this problem and take the steps necessary to recover from it.

What I would like to look at next are some of the concepts about what causes alcoholism and addiction.

Nature Versus Nurture

There is an ongoing dispute in the treatment community over whether addiction is a genetic issue more than a psychological issue. So, is it *nature* or is it *nurture*?

Nature

There seems to be growing evidence that people who suffer from addictions, especially alcoholism, have a genetic predisposition to this disease. This could explain the higher-than-normal incidents of children of alcoholics becoming alcoholics themselves. There has been research that indicated that the livers of alcoholics may metabolize alcohol differently than non-alcoholics. If this is true, this would explain why some people cannot "hold their liquor." If someone's liver metabolized alcohol more slowly, that would leave the effects of alcohol more prevalent in that person for a longer period of time. So, someone who drank too much would still be under the influence of alcohol some time later, while someone with a normal liver would have already metabolized the alcohol from his system.

There was also research that pointed out that certain subgroups, or sections of society, are more predisposed to alcoholism than others. However, this wouldn't explain why some children of alcoholics, and other members of the subgroups, do not become alcoholics.

Nurture

The idea that addiction is a learned behavior has merit and believability in both the scientific and lay community. It also helps explain why children of alcoholics, for instance, are more predisposed to becoming alcoholics. Children of addicts learn the behavior and see it as normal, so the behavior becomes theirs. They also may learn, in this environment, that some of the problems and dysfunction that come with alcohol or drug abuse are normal and to be expected. In that case, even problems that might cause someone from a non-addict background to stop using—things like fighting, missing work, neglecting family responsibilities, financial difficulties, and legal issues related to use—would be considered normal.

At the same time, the question of whether alcoholism and other addictions are genetic or learned really is a side issue. It has no bearing on recovery. In fact, too many people get so caught up looking for the cause that they miss sight of looking for the solution.

Behavior

Many in the treatment community now look at drinking, drug abuse and other addictions as more of a behavior issue. If one can alter the behavior, then one would stop the abuse of alcohol or drugs. That's easier to say than to do, however. The behavior is quite complex.

When you look at addictions as behaviors, you must look at the entire landscape of the person who is exhibiting the behavior. Substance abuse does not occur in a vacuum. Many people only use alcohol or drugs in social situations, such as at a party or in a bar. Others, however, may only use the drug or pursue the behavior at home, hiding their addiction from the world. Some who are addicted to food may eat only a few bites in a restaurant, but then return home and gorge themselves.

When it comes to alcoholism, it's not unusual to see someone who drinks normally in public, having only a couple of drinks at a party or other social setting, but who, at home, drinks like an alcoholic. Those of us who work with alcoholics have seen this phenomenon increase with the crackdown on drunk driving. It's also a defense mechanism to keep others from seeing the person drink too much. This is the type of person who, after a couple of drinks at a social event, can't wait to get home to finish drinking. They may be able to control their drinking to some extent, but they definitely have a problem.

We also see some who drink rarely at home, but who will overindulge when placed in a social situation. They get drunk at parties, weddings, and other social gatherings but rarely get drunk at home.

Again, I have to stress that it's not *what* you use, or *when* you use it, it's *what it does to you.* Some addicts only use in public and other addicts only use at home, but the common factor is the behavior. If the addiction, and the behaviors associated with it, is causing problems, then the behavior must be altered to stop the problems.

I've worked with many clients who drank too much at home for years and never thought of it as a problem until they started to drink more in public. Many times family members and loved ones will protect such alcoholics by mistakenly thinking that, by having them only drink at home, they are helping them. Usually, after they start the recovery process, alcoholics' family members will tell them that their drinking bothered them for years.

Mindscape

Some of the more cutting-edge information in addictions has to do with the idea that the addiction is a brain-based issue. This has to do with the neurotransmitters (or brain chemicals) dopamine and serotonin. When these neurotransmitters are out of balance, it's easy for one to self-medicate using alcohol or another drug of choice.

In the treatment community, the idea of a client self-medicating has been around for years. We see people return to their addictions for many reasons, usually as a form of stress relief or a way to relieve a physical, mental or emotional pain. Seemingly, addicts train their brains to rely on the drug or behavior to help them biobalance these brain chemicals. (This topic will be covered more in-depth in the obsession and compulsion chapter.)

So, as we look at who is an addict, I stress that you don't get caught up in labels. Just use the information to make your life better. On the following pages, you'll find some of questions from current literature that you can answer for yourself.

ALCOHOL IN YOUR LIFE.....

How Important Is It?

MAST	Yes	No
1. Do you feel you are a normal drinker? (If you deny any use of alcohol, check here.)		
2. Have you ever awakened the morning after some drinking the night before and found that you could not remember a part of the evening prior?		
3. Does your spouse (or parents) ever worry or complain about your drinking?		
4. Can you stop drinking without a struggle after one or two drinks?		
5. Do you ever feel bad about your drinking?		
6. Do friends or relatives think you are a normal drinker?		
7. Do you ever try to limit your drinking to certain times of the day or to certain places?		
8. Are you always able to stop drinking when you want to?		
9. Have you ever attended a meeting of Alcoholics Anonymous (A.A.)?		
10. Have you ever gotten into fights when drinking?		
11. Has drinking ever created problems with you and your spouse?		

MAST	Yes	No
12. Has your spouse (or other family member) ever gone for help about your drinking?		
13. Have you ever lost friends or girlfriends/boyfriends because of drinking?		
14. Have you ever gotten into trouble at work because of drinking?		
15. Have you ever lost a job because of drinking?		
16. Have you ever neglected your obligations, your family, or your work for two or more days in a row because you were drinking?		
17. Do you ever drink before noon?		
18. Have you ever been told you have liver trouble? Cirrhosis?		
19. Have you ever had delirium tremens (DTs), severe shaking, heard voices, or seen things that weren't there after heavy drinking?		
20. Have you ever gone to anyone for help about your drinking?		
21. Have you ever been in a hospital because of drinking?		
22. Have you ever been a patient in a psychiatric hospital or on a psychiatric ward of a general hospital where drinking was a part of the problem?		

MAST Answers		
1.	No	2
2.	Yes	2
3.	Yes	1
4.	No	2
5.	Yes	1
6.	No	2
7.	Yes	0
8.	No	2
9.	Yes	5
10.	Yes	1
11.	Yes	2
12.	Yes	2
13.	Yes	2
14.	Yes	2
15.	Yes	2
16.	Yes	2
17.	Yes	1
18.	Yes	2
19.	Yes	2
20.	Yes	5
21.	Yes	5
22.	Yes	2

0-7 —— No Problem
8-15 —— Alcohol Abuse
15+ —— Alcoholism

JHU	Yes	No
1. Do you require a drink in the morning?		
2. Do you prefer (or like) to drink alone?		
3. Do you lose time from work due to drinking?		
4. Is your drinking harming your family in any way?		
5. Do you crave a drink at a definite time daily?		
6. Do you get the inner shakes unless you continue drinking?		
7. Has drinking made you irritable?		
8. Does drinking make you careless of your family's welfare?		
9. Have you thought less of your husband or wife since drinking?		
10. Has drinking changed your personality?		
11. Does drinking cause you bodily complaints?		
12. Does drinking cause you to have difficulty in sleeping?		
13. Has drinking made you more impulsive?		
14. Have you less self-control since drinking?		
15. Has your initiative decreased since drinking?		
16. Has your ambition decreased since drinking?		

JHU	Yes	No
17. Do you drink to obtain social ease?		
18. Do you drink for self-encouragement or to relieve marked feelings of inadequacy?		
19. Has your sexual potency suffered since drinking?		
20. Do you show marked dislikes and hatreds since drinking?		
21. Has your jealousy, in general, increased since drinking?		
22. Do you show marked moodiness as a result of drinking?		
23. Has your efficiency decreased since drinking?		
24. Are you harder to get along with since drinking?		
25. Do you turn to an inferior environment since drinking?		
26. Is drinking endangering your health?		
27. Is drinking affecting your peace of mind?		
28. Is drinking jeopardizing your business?		
29. Is drinking clouding your reputation?		
30. Have you ever had a complete loss of memory while, or after drinking?		

Current Treatments

These days, there's a lot of work and research going into treating the health problems that result from addictions. That's understandable, since addiction presents a serious health problem, not just here in the United States, but globally. In fact, tobacco and alcohol are ranked fourth and fifth among risk factors for disease around the world. Abuse of those two substances alone is thought to be involved in over 6.7 million deaths per year worldwide…and that's not counting other forms of addiction.

Unfortunately, there are fewer resources available when it comes to helping people quit before health problems become irreversible. The treatment that is available for most forms of addiction usually involves several methods, including detoxification, a 12-step group, family therapy, group therapy or vocational counseling. Usually, the first step is breaking through the person's denial, since denial is common with all kinds of addictions. Studies done in the area of alcohol addiction have also shown that emotions are key in how an addict approaches recovery and, therefore, how successful that person is in breaking the addiction for good.

As we look at the current treatments for addictions, the two most dominant are psychotherapy and therapeutic approaches using a 12-step model. Many treatment centers use a combination of these two with some aspects of a medical model.

Therapy

The psychotherapy model varies according to the style of the psychotherapist. It's been shown, though, that any successful treatment needs to help the addict overcome feelings of anger or impulsivity and help the person maintain a more serene feeling. Once that happens, the person is much more likely to commit to his or her recovery.

Therapy models include classical psychoanalytic methods such as Freud or Jung, rational-emotive therapy, and cognitive-behavioral therapy. All of these therapies work on restructuring how a person thinks and reacts to the addiction. All such methods work to some extent, but success really depends on getting the right pair of methods at the right time for the right client. Unfortunately, this is often a matter of luck more than anything else.

Cognitive-Behavioral Therapy

The most common therapy currently used for addictions is cognitive-behavioral, which attacks both the thought processes—the thoughts, feelings and emotions about the addiction—and the behavior of the addiction. The cognitive-behavioral approach fits in well with the 12-step or medical models. There are many books written on this approach to helping people change.

Disease Model

This popular model is used in many treatment programs, including A.A. The disease model believes that addiction is a biological disease that affects only certain people. In a way, addiction is determined by the luck of the draw. Those who follow the disease model believe addiction is genetic and that addicts may, in fact, be physically different from other people.

Denial is considered part of the disease, so programs that follow the disease model tend to confront the problem in order to break through denial. Those who have the disease of addiction experience loss of control. Inevitably, addiction leads to death, institutionalization or sobriety. Followers of the disease model also believe the addiction is transferable to another substance, though I don't find that the research necessarily supports this.

Finally, lifetime abstinence is considered the only way to solve the addiction. According to the disease model, there is no cure, only the process.

Adaptive Model

The adaptive model believes addiction may or may not be genetic. It sees addictive behavior as a way to solve life problems. For instance, if a person is feeling stress, the behavior may relieve stress for a short time. The adaptive model believes there is a fine line between use and addiction.

Followers of this model believe people develop severe drug problems because they're trying to compensate for shortcomings such as shyness, uncontrollable stress or an inferiority complex. The adaptive model believes you can understand addiction the same way you can understand other maladaptive behaviors. Programs that use this model concentrate on the person's thoughts.

Abstinence may be a goal, but it's not the only goal. A lot of people who follow this model believe you can turn addicts into "social users," though I've never seen it done successfully. They also approach treatment slowly. As you can see, this method is in direct conflict with the disease model.

Harm/Risk Reduction Model

This model's focus is on the harm done, not on the drug or behavior itself. The thinking is that we all engage in some high-risk behaviors, of which addiction is simply one. The goal of this method is to lower the harm caused by the high-risk behavior or addiction. For instance, if a person is an alcoholic and drives drunk, the focus is to stop the drunk driving, not necessarily to stop all drinking.

Believers in the harm/risk reduction model say there are both biological and psycho-social factors to addiction; addiction is a maladaptive behavior, they say, not a disease. In this model, *any* lowering of use is considered a success.

Medical

The medical model uses a medical approach based in psychotropic medication. Our culture is always looking for a "magic bullet"—a medicine, a pill or a shot—that will cure an addiction or relieve cravings. Antidepressants, mood elevators, selective serotonin re-uptake inhibitors, and central nervous system depressants (i.e., valium) are some of the medications the medical model uses in a search for such a magic bullet.

One current trend leans toward using a drug to block the pleasure sensation that the addictive substance or behavior gives to the addict. It's thought that, by removing the pleasure received, a person will stop abusing and using the drug. This method has had some success, but it always brings up the question of *what happens when one stops taking the drug that blocks the pleasure.* If one has not fixed the cause of the addiction, doesn't it make sense that the person would drink or take the drug again? After all, the underlying reasons and behaviors haven't changed.

NLP Process of Addictions

We'll cover the Neuro-Linguistic Programming (NLP) process of addictions in more detail later. After all, it's largely what this book is based on! Briefly though, NLP believes there may be a genetic link to addiction, but is open to the idea that there may not be. NLP uses the "iceberg" approach to addiction and treatment...we know that only 10-12% of brain function is conscious. All the real motivation, both toward addiction and toward a healthy life, happens under the surface. It that 88-90% on which we focus.

Alcoholics Anonymous

The greatest step in addiction treatment happened in 1935 with the advent of Alcoholics Anonymous (A.A.). Alcoholics Anonymous uses a self-monitoring and peer-based approach to helping people change. It's a step-by-step (thus the 12 steps) approach to changing a person's thoughts and behaviors about the addiction. Most people don't realize the background of A.A., but Alcoholics Anonymous has an interesting past. So, as we look at some of the treatments available today, let's also glance at some of the history of alcoholism and treatments here in the United States.

History

Abstinence

One of the signers of the Declaration of Independence was Dr. Benjamin Rush. Rush was a practicing physician in the mid-1700s who talked about alcohol as a problem in our new country. He wrote that certain people simply shouldn't drink. They couldn't handle alcohol; they reacted differently from normal drinkers. Rush proposed that the only treatment for this problem was total abstinence…yet he gave no way for the person to achieve this goal.

In 1813 the temperance movement was growing in our new country. The temperance movement focused on gin and the social problems related to drinking, and suggested that people temper, or reduce, their drinking. It was a worthwhile movement, yet they still offered no way to achieve this goal.

Spirituality

In 1826, a fundamentalist preacher named Lyman Beecher referred to people who drank too much as suffering from moral weakness and sinful behavior. Beecher suggested total abstinence. He had no plan to help people remain abstinent, but it's thought he suggested praying for help. This led to the idea that if you couldn't maintain total abstinence, then you were sinful and morally weak. The connection between drinking and sin and moral weakness became prevalent in our moral culture here in the United States, and throughout the Western world.

In 1840, a new movement appeared. This new movement was the Washingtonian movement. The Washingtonian movement also thought drinking was a moral problem, and its members suggested total abstinence, but they gave a plan to help. The plan was fellowship with other people who were attempting to remain abstinent from alcohol. This movement became huge in the United States. In fact, at the outbreak of the Civil War, it's estimated that there were several hundred thousand members of the Washingtonian movement. Unfortunately, it got involved in politics. The same issues that divided America also broke up the Washingtonian movement.

The turn of the twentieth century saw a time of rapid expansion and the acceptance of psychology as a science. In 1900, there was a psychological movement that stressed having a spiritual experience to help one overcome the use of alcohol. However, this movement had no path to help people remain abstinent, other than through such a spiritual experience.

In 1928, the Oxford Group, named after the railroad car in which people would meet to talk about ways to remain abstinent from alcohol, was growing and expanding. Members of the Oxford Group still thought of drinking as a sin. They also thought the only way to recover was through spiritual experience. However, the Oxford Group was the first group to develop a step-by-step plan to help people achieve this spiritual experience and remain alcohol-free. They had a six-step program that used fellowship with other members and specific steps to guide people on the spiritual path.

Bill Wilson and Alcoholics Anonymous

In the early 1930s, Bill Wilson, the founder of Alcoholics Anonymous, was trying to quit drinking. He'd tried just about everything. He'd even gone to Europe to consult Dr. Carl Jung. Jung had expressed the thought that only a spiritual experience that produced a complete psychic change would help someone stop drinking. It's thought he suggested the Oxford Group to Wilson.

In 1934, a member of the Oxford Group visited Bill Wilson and talked to him about a recovery program to help him stop drinking. Wilson followed the advice and followed the steps, and was sober for several months. Then he went on a business trip to Akron Ohio.

The Ohio business trip did not go well. Wilson was despondent and, while in the lobby of his hotel, he heard the music and laughter from the bar. He wanted to go into the bar and look for comfort. He had no one from the Oxford Group to talk to as he would normally do in such a situation. Before he went into the bar, however, he saw a list of local churches. He randomly called the first church from the list and asked the minister if any of his flock needed help with their drinking. The minister gave him Dr. Bob Smith's phone number. Doctor Bob, the other cofounder of Alcoholics Anonymous, was at that time in the process of drinking and ruining his life.

Bill Wilson visited Doctor Bob and shared with him his experiences and strengthened hope. He offered Doctor Bob a way out. Wilson stayed in Ohio for several weeks and helped Doctor Bob on his path to sobriety. From this chance meeting, A.A. grew into the worldwide phenomenon it is today.

As I said before, I believe the single most important event to take place in the field of alcoholism treatment was the 1939 publication of *Alcoholics Anonymous,* sometimes called *The Big Book.* When the people whom we call "the first 100" began to realize that their method of recovery was effective, they decided that the things they had learned might be helpful to others, so they placed their experiences in a book. This textbook contained the first definitive program for diagnosing and treating the disease of alcoholism. As this information spread across the country, more people joined the program and used the recovery methods described to recover from alcoholism.

The 12-step program Wilson and Smith developed was intended to help people get on with normal life. It was never intended to become a life unto itself. Rather, the 12 steps are a bridge back to normal living.

Government Programs

In 1970, the federal government became involved in solving the problem of alcoholism in the United States. This was the first time a major country had decided to dedicate its efforts to combating alcohol abuse. Projects were begun all over the country. These government-funded alcoholism treatment projects involved people from many different fields. Most were from the mental health and social work professions. However, there were also many recovered alcoholics, whose only background in the treatment field was their own recovery.

Until 1970, the A.A. program had been the single method that had successfully treated the disease of alcoholism. The variety of educational and vocational backgrounds among the new workers, and the different methods and techniques these workers introduced, caused a lot of confusion in this new field. Their methods achieved varying degrees of success, but each also experienced a lot of discouraging failure. The failure was largely caused by a lack of understanding in how to treat alcoholics. Even today, the people working in this field are pioneers in the field of alcoholism as a public health problem. They are blazing a trail for people yet to come.

Most treatment centers provide excellent care for the alcoholic, but many offer everything to the clients except a program designed to bring about recovery. Most of America's treatment centers have no consistent procedures for treating alcoholism. Right now, treatment is designed according to the concepts of each treatment center. How the counselors in those centers are trained is sometimes determined by the lifestyle of the particular city, state, or region where the program is being implemented. Because of the widespread variation among treatment procedures and methods, you never quite know what you're going to get when you walk into a treatment center.

None of this is meant to take away from the great strides that have been made in the treatment of addictions. Each of the treatments listed here works in its own way. The trick is to figure out which program, or parts of programs, works best for you.

That's what I've tried to do with the Apex Program. I've taken what I believe is the best from each method and left the rest. Together, we'll cross that bridge out of addiction and back to normal life. It's time to get on with your life.

Obsession & Compulsion: Failure Happens

Now that we've looked at some of the current treatments, it's time to look at the *why*. Why is my craving running my life? What caused it? Why is it so hard to get rid of it?

When a person is addicted to a substance or behavior, nothing else matters. All you can think about is taking a hit, getting a drag, finding that next drink. You only know that you need to eat that snack, play those slots, or find that sexual partner. In *The Craving Brain*, Dr. Ruden calls this feeling "Gotta have it." As an addict, that's what your brain tells you. "I have to have it, and I have to have it *now*." Family, finances, health and sanity…all take second place to your compulsion.

No matter what the addiction, the common threads are your inability to resist it and your inability to stop the behavior. This inability most likely makes you feel powerless and inadequate, which only strengthens the addiction's hold on your life. It's like slavery or, as one addict said, as if someone else is bending you to their will.

This chapter isn't meant to be a biology lesson, but biology may help you understand the *why*. Ultimately, your addiction is about your drive to survive. Survival is biological. That's what makes it nearly impossible to overcome.

When you suffer from an addiction, your brain sends out the message that you have to have this substance, or die. This doesn't make sense to most of us when it comes to an addiction. Why would I need a piece of chocolate cake…or a cigarette…or a one-night stand?

It's All about Biology

Deep in your brain, underneath and beyond your conscious thought or will, is an area that controls your survival. That's all this part of the brain cares about. To ensure survival of the species, your brain alters the levels of your brain chemicals, called*neurochemicals* and *glucortoids*, to spur you to act for your own survival. In an addict, abnormal levels of those brain chemicals seem to keep the person in constant survival mode.

That's why an addict often reacts to a compulsion as if his or her life is at stake. The brain thinks it is. When the obsession seems to be a matter of survival, a person will do nearly anything to satisfy it. That's when you drive for hours to go to a casino, venture to a dangerous part of town for a drug or prostitute, or wipe out a child's college fund to pay for a habit. You'll do anything to survive.

A Question of Survival

The question of why we're here may seem philosophical, but the answer is partly biological. We're here because we survived. We're here because our parents survived, and our grandparents, and every generation back to the beginning. Nature gave us great tools to help us survive, both our visible bodies—hands, feet, eyes, noses—and our internal processes.

One of those internal tools is our limbic system. Also known as the reptilian brain, the limbic system today provides functions for survival much as it did eons ago. It's what drives your survival behaviors, including those obsessions and compulsions related to your addiction. Want, need and desire are all normal responses in certain circumstances. Obsession happens when survival is at stake.

Historically, the limbic system drives three main behaviors: eating, avoiding being eaten, and reproducing. Those behaviors may look very different than they did generations ago, but the purpose is the same. You got it. *Survival.*

Your limbic system gathers input from your senses, then sends messages to an area called the nucleus accumbens. Your nucleus accumbens gathers information from your limbic system and several other areas of the brain. When it decides what you need to do for your survival, it produces the matching response and tells your body, "Go get it!"

It sends this signal through a brain chemical called *dopamine*. Dopamine is the "have to have it" signal. It's the chemical that raises our awareness and focuses our attention. It makes us alert and aids in learning. Dopamine levels are highest when you're actively seeking what you need for survival.

If dopamine is the "have to have it" signal, *serotonin* signals "got it." Once you've fulfilled that urgent need, the brain releases serotonin, the chemical that lets the body know that the hunger has been sated, that you're safe, that you're satisfied. Serotonin is the brain chemical that soothes us and lowers our ability to focus. Serotonin is also what your body needs when it's overwhelmed by too much information at once.

Needs Aren't Debatable

Your survival needs aren't debatable. That's because nature chose pain as both a teacher and a motivator. Imagine that it's close to lunch time, but you're deeply involved in a project. Your brain starts sending your body signals that you're hungry. You experience the first rumblings in your stomach. For a while, you can ignore those signals. Eventually, though, they become too severe to ignore. That's because, to your brain, hunger is not debatable! It's a matter of survival, and your body will do whatever it takes to motivate you to get food.

The same thing happens with your safety or your drive to procreate. Your brain drives you to seek out the herd for safety, or to find a mate to further the species. The signals start out small, but finally become too severe to ignore.

Hunger, anxiety and longing all create stress. They disturb the balance, or *homeostasis,* in our bodies. When that balance is disturbed, we focus our attention on the thing we need in order to restore balance. Dopamine levels skyrocket, and we seek the substance or behavior that we subconsciously know will raise our serotonin. With an addiction, the brain sends the mistaken, but still painfully urgent, message that we have to have that drug or pursue that behavior to restore balance.

It's only when dopamine and serotonin levels are both high that you experience a sense of contentment. Your body is in a state of harmony, of balance. Nothing more needs to be done for your survival. This is the goal of all motivated behavior. Understanding this process—both what drives our need and what it takes to reach that balance—will lead you to the end of your addiction.

Nature + Nurture + Anchor + Beliefs = Addiction

When you look at this new information about how the brain gets out of balance, you understand the physical aspect of obsession and compulsion. However, that explains only part of the complexity of recovery.

When you have the genetic quirk of the craving/compulsion response, it doesn't normally reset when you get the object that started the dopamine spike. Rather than sending the "Got it" signal, the first drink spurs the craving for a second, and so on. Then you bring in some beliefs about the behavior in an attempt to cope. "Real men can control their liquor." "I deserve this drink (fix, chocolate, etc.)" Those beliefs simply add to the behavior; they make the behavior seem normal.

Triggers—seeing people partying, a song that brings back memories of a fun time drinking or getting high, seeing a late night ad for food—can start or continue the addiction cycle. This may explain the cycles we get into with our addictions.

The Structure of a Binge

When we talk about recovery from an addiction, it's also important to think about the process of binging. When you experience obsession or compulsion, the habit you're trying to stop is also the only behavior you feel driven to do to relieve your suffering (dopamine spike) so you can feel temporary relief (the serotonin).

It becomes a vicious cycle. You give in to the craving, but then you feel guilty because you're trying to stop this destructive habit. The guilt raises your dopamine and you feel worse. The only behavior you know that will bring relief is the behavior that causes the problem. So, you drink or use the drug or fall into the behavior again, feel worse and repeat the whole process.

The behavior that causes the guilt and remorse is the only behavior we know of that brings relief.

The only way out of this cycle is to learn a new way to reset your brain. You need to restructure the neurons in your brain so you can react in a new way. This is what psychotherapy tries to do. It's what 12-step programs teach in a round-about way, and what medication attempts to accomplish. Want to know a secret? Meditation, hypnosis, NLP and guided imagery can all help you achieve this. Every other form of treatment tries this, but few get the key. In this program, I've given you the key.

Change your mental processes, your beliefs, and your actions will change. The relief you desire will be yours. The craving, obsessions and compulsions will fade away!

All you need to do is retrain your brain.

The Illusion of Control

What do I mean by the illusion of control?

The illusion of control is the paradox of realizing that true control comes from accepting that many things are beyond our control. The economy, weather and world situations...all will do what they will. They don't ask our permission, and they don't need our help.

We all strive for control in small areas of our lives, especially when we feel that the major areas are beyond our control. This is particularly present in alcoholics and addicts. We strive to control the one thing that we falsely believe will give us pleasure or bring relief to our emotional pain. This is true whether we suffer from anorexia, trying to control our bodies when our lives make no sense, or whether we immerse ourselves in drugs in an attempt to get "high" or dull the pain. After all, isn't that all we really control... ourselves?

The problem is, when we seek control through addiction, it's the substance or behavior that's really in control. In order to regain control, we have to learn to control our internal states and internal reactions (reaction is the ability to act). As a great leader once said "The kingdom of heaven is within" (Luke 17:21). We have to learn a new ability, the ability to have internal, or subconscious, control. The Neuro Restructuring Technique using NLP and hypnosis does just that. This is the key, the foundation on which all recovery is based: reprogramming the mind!

Here is some text from the classic work in the field of addictions:

MORE ABOUT ALCOHOLISM*

Most of us have been unwilling to admit we were real alcoholics. No person likes to think he is bodily and mentally different from his fellows. Therefore, it is not surprising that our drinking careers have been characterized by countless vain attempts to prove we could drink like other people. The idea that somehow, someday he will control and enjoy his drinking is the great obsession of every abnormal drinker. The persistence of this illusion is astonishing. Many pursue it into the gates of insanity or death.

We learned that we had to fully concede to our innermost selves that we were alcoholics. This is the first step in recovery. The delusion that we are like other people, or presently may be, has to be smashed.

We alcoholics are men and women who have lost the ability to control our drinking. We know that no real alcoholic ever recovers control. All of us felt at times that we were regaining control, but such intervals - usually brief - were inevitably followed by still less control, which led in time to pitiful and incomprehensible demoralization. We are convinced to a man that alcoholics of our type are in the grip of a progressive illness. Over any considerable period we get worse, never better.

We are like men who have lost their legs; they never grow new ones. Neither does there appear to be any kind of treatment which will make alcoholics of our kind like other men. We have tried every imaginable remedy. In some instances there has been brief recovery, followed always by a still worse relapse. Physicians who are familiar with alcoholism agree there is no such thing as making a normal drinker out of an alcoholic. Science may one day accomplish this, but it hasn't done so yet.

Despite all we can say, many who are real alcoholics are not going to believe they are in that class. By every form of self-deception and experimentation, they will try to prove themselves exceptions to the rule, therefore nonalcoholic. If anyone who is showing inability to control his drinking can do the right-about-face and drink like a gentleman, our hats are off to him. Heaven knows, we have tried hard enough and long enough to drink like other people!

Here are some of the methods we have tried: Drinking beer only, limiting the number of drinks, never drinking alone, never drinking in the morning, drinking only at home, never having it in the house, never drinking during business hours, drinking only at parties, switching from scotch to brandy, drinking only natural wines, agreeing to resign if ever drunk on the job, taking a trip, not taking a trip, swearing off forever (with and without a solemn oath), taking more physical exercise, reading inspirational books, going to health farms and sanitariums, accepting voluntary commitment to asylums - we could increase the list ad infinitum.

*From *Alcoholics Anonymous, The Big Book*, p 30-31.

We all strive for that sense of control, but the paradox again is about our perception. Addiction creates a false sense of control.

Your Life Is How You Perceive It !!!

Life can be as big and important as you make it. Or it can be as small and insignificant as you make it. I'm talking about, "Life is what you perceive it as," which has a lot to do with the classic dismissal, "It's all relative."

Some people see life as grand and multifaceted. They recognize so much to see and do, so many things going on in the world around them. One person could never keep track of it all, or do everything that could be done, in one lifetime.

Others take the opposite viewpoint. They see life as inconsequential. Nothing they do seems to matter much. Although there are a lot of people in the world, none of them seems to be doing anything particularly important or interesting; they just go about their daily tasks of living. No matter how you live your life, such a person thinks, eventually it will end, and the world at large will not have changed much for it.

Both viewpoints are correct. That's right; *both* are correct. It all has to do with how you see things. Some people like to see things as big and complex, while others see things as small and simple.

Situational Perception

What kind of world do you live in? What kind of people do you surround yourself with, fearful people or loving people? Do you react to situations in life fearfully or lovingly?

How you *react* to life determines how your world will continue to be. How you*perceive* that world determines how your world will continue to be.

What kind of world does "you" live in...a world of competition and survival or a world of love, abundance, prosperity and cooperation? Do you live in hell on earth or heaven on earth? What level of consciousness does "you" perceive life's challenges through: victim consciousness, where things happen to you, or mastery consciousness, where you make things happen?

All things, all experiences, all challenges, all relationships, can be perceived differently at those different levels of consciousness. What might seem like a negative situation at a "victim" level can be experienced as a positive in a higher state of consciousness. It can be an experience of growth, of greater awareness and of greater development of loving abilities, such as a greater compassion and understanding.

You are NOT OK; I am NOT OK

You've probably heard the mantra, "I'm okay; you're okay." Many people, though, perceive life much differently. For instance, how do people handle the following situations in their lives?

Guilt

Each of us has incidents in our lives that, were we given the chance, we would probably handle differently. This is only natural. We're all human. As the poet, Alexander Pope, said, "To err is human, to forgive divine." To be human is to make mistakes. No one is immune. No one is perfect.

It's healthy to let go of your past mistakes and errors in judgment, learning whatever lessons need to be learned from those experiences. Unfortunately, many of us replay past mistakes and beat ourselves up over and over again. To hold yourself responsible in this way, and to live with guilt daily, is to be trapped in the past. This vicious cycle of self-abasement cuts off our life force and weakens us.

Hate

Hate is one of the most toxic forms of energy, and you should avoid it at all costs. Hate, whether it is self-hate or directed towards another, almost always causes serious illness to those who foolishly indulge in its cesspool energy. I don't care how justified you feel you are in hating another individual; you do so at your own risk.

Think about how you feel when you hate. Take a minute right now and spend 60 seconds thinking about someone you dislike. Really get into it and hate that person for a full 60 seconds, and then observe how you feel when you're finished. Why would you want that energy in you on a regular basis? Be aware that your hate doesn't adversely affect the person you're hating…it affects you.

Self-Pity

Every life has things that are happy and things that are unhappy. If you want to feel sorry for yourself, you only have to look at your life to discover many reasons to be unhappy. Likewise, if you want to feel gratitude for what's happening in your life, there are many reasons to be thankful. It's your choice how you perceive your life. If you choose self-pity, even if you have the right to choose it, self-pity will cause unhappiness.

I'm not suggesting that you go around trying to be happy every moment of every day. Nor am I suggesting a Pollyanna perspective that ignores the sometimes-harsh realties of life. No life is ideal. We all have crises and issues that are unpleasant.

If you want to feel depressed or indulge in self-pity, why not give yourself an afternoon and really get into it. Sometimes this can act as a healthy release, so go ahead. Wallow in your misery; feel how truly rotten and miserable your life is. Then, when you're finished, let go of your misery and move on. To indulge daily in self-pity will make it a habit that will leak your life force from you.

Fear and Worry

Fear and worry are mind power techniques in reverse. Whatever you fear and worry about, you attract. I know that's unfair, but it's the truth. It's the law of our being. Avoid the bad habits of fear and worry. Train your mind to focus on what you want to happen, rather than imagining what you don't want happening. It's so obvious and simple, and yet many people fall into these bad mental habits and suffer the consequences, both internal and external.

When you understand life force in this way, you have an added reason to be aware of your thoughts. We now realize that negative states of mind not only affect our success, but also our wellness and ability to perform at our best. Our very essence and being is affected by how we think and feel.

Conclusion

Your experience of life so far has been proof that the agreed-upon human reality was real. Underneath it all, though, you knew there was something better. This knowing was your true self, urging you on to truth, urging you on to live in heaven instead of hell. This was your awakening. Now you must realize that heaven on earth is created by the perception that this heaven is real, rather than the illusionary hell within which you have existed.

Everyone needs to come to the point where they realize they are not victims to anyone or anything. You need to realize that your individual experience of heaven is completely in your control, solely based on how you perceive it. You are indeed the master of your reality. I know it appears otherwise, but this is a temporary condition that fades upon your ascension to higher conscious awareness. Then the pieces of the puzzle all start to fit. All the random elements that have occurred in your life become specific and meaningful…meaningful to your spiritual growth.

The big picture is that life is always expanding, and growing. We're always creating new things for our experience. We're always creating more self. Through limitation, through all degrees and dimensions of physical expression, we experience more of self. This is also a paradox, a paradox I recommend not trying to solve.

Who's in Control? Your Conscious versus Subconscious

Think of yourself as having basically two minds: your conscious mind and your subconscious mind. Your conscious mind is your thinking, awake state of awareness, yet it comprises a paltry 12% of your mind. You make changes and break free from addictions when you bypass that 12% of your mind that's conscious and get to the real power center…you subconscious.

First, though, let's look at your conscious mind. Your conscious mind has five functions:

1. **Analysis**
2. **Rationalization**
3. **Willpower**

4. **Functional memory**
5. **Voluntary body functions**

1. Analysis: Your conscious mind is logical because it is analytical. Its job is to study the problems you have and solve them.

2. Rationalization: This part of your mind tells you why you do things, gives you reasons to do things and helps you understand why you do things. The problem is, it's usually wrong! True motivation for behavior comes from a much deeper part of our mind that we don't normally have access to with our conscious mind. For instance, you might say you smoke because it relaxes you. That's not really why—after all, a hot bath or some deep breathing would also relax you—but it's the rationalization that your brain tells you. It's a tidy, neat, logical answer. Not complete and certainly not correct, but logical.

3. Willpower: This is what makes you stop and think before doing something.

Unfortunately, your conscious mind isn't very good at this function. If it were, you wouldn't need this book, because you could simply *will* yourself to stop using!

4. Functional Memory: The short-term memory, our functioning memory, is usually all we need to get through life. That's why, even though in third grade you needed to know how to get from your classroom to the bathroom, decades later you can't even remember where your third grade classroom was. The brain drops (but doesn't totally "lose") the stuff we don't need in order to survive on a day-to-day basis.

5. Voluntary Body Functions: As long as you aren't physically impaired by injury, illness, or other physical condition, your brain tells your legs, "Hey, let's go," or tells your hand to keep away from that hot stove. If you tried to control your internal bodily functions that are normally on autopilot, though—like digestion and blood pressure—you normally can't unless you access them through some form of hypnosis. Remember, your conscious mind makes up approximately 12% of your entire mind. That's not a lot! So, there must be some pretty exciting stuff going on somewhere else. In order to finally break your habit and live the life you want to live, you need to learn how to communicate with that part of your mind.

So, you can see that the key to making any major change lies in your subconscious mind. That 88% of your mind is the power center; it's the motherboard of your body. Just like with a computer, as long as it's working properly, you never know it's there. If it wasn't there, though, nothing else could happen. Its single most significant characteristic is that *it literally runs your life without you knowing it.* The problem is that many people spend too much time listening to that loud and obnoxious 12% instead of tapping into the true power center. Like an iceberg, the subconscious is hidden beneath deep, dark waters, with only a small part showing on the surface.

Our mind was meant to function differently, but we don't understand it. We're like monkeys pounding away on a keyboard with no comprehension as to how the computer works. Sometimes the monkey gets lucky and something good happens. The truth is, it's just a matter of knowing which keys to press.

The keys are simple:

- **The subconscious mind cannot think, reason, or argue.** So what does it do? It FEELS.
- **The subconscious mind is the emotional center of your being.** Control your emotions, and you control YOURSELF. Many times, your emotions are out of sight, buried beneath your conscious mind or disguised by rationalization.
- **Your subconscious mind controls who you are, how you respond, and what you believe.** You generally don't stop and think about your beliefs when you pour another drink or reach for your fourth brownie, but your responses are usually based upon your belief system.
- **Your habits are a function of your subconscious mind.** When you repeat the same action over and over, eventually it will become a habit. A habit is an automatic response. It's an action that starts in the conscious mind and, through repetition, shifts into the realm of the subconscious...like using a turn signal or checking to make sure you have your keys before you lock the door.
- **The subconscious mind is a huge storage unit for all memories, thoughts, dreams, fantasies and experiences, whether real or imagined.** Your subconscious simply records everything; it doesn't make judgments as to reality.
- **The subconscious protects you from real and imagined dangers.** This is good because it keeps you safe, but bad because it's how phobias and addictions take root.

You're probably beginning to see a little more about what I mean when I talk about the "illusion" of control. With all this going on underneath the surface, are you really in control if you only use that 12% of your brain?

The good news here is that your conscious and subconscious minds work together. Your subconscious mind holds all your long-term memories, and while it influences how your conscious mind works and acts, it can be reprogrammed to do what you want it to do.

The conscious mind is the active master; it thinks, perceives, exerts will, is aware, instigates activity and can be objective.

The subconscious mind acts like a servant, but is really the *cause* of who you are. It controls your feelings, blindly records your experiences and thoughts, is the source of your personal power and is totally subjective.

Overcoming addiction is about taking control of your subconscious mind. This is powerful, because if a suggestion is allowed to travel from your conscious to your subconscious mind, then it has the power to change your beliefs and behaviors.

First, though, a suggestion has to make it through the critical factor of your conscious mind. That's the part of your conscious mind that works to protect the status quo of your subconscious mind. It's the part of you that keeps you from believing every single thing you're told. It acts as a filter to make sure what you're hearing is in agreement with what's already stored.

How can you break through that filter to get through to the subconscious mind? In this book, and even more in the Apex Program, I'll show you how to bypass the critical factor of your conscious mind to allow you to access the subconscious and focus your mind to accept new, positive information. You'll be able to leave yourself wide open to the suggestion that you can function as a whole, happy person without the need for the negative behavior that's been holding you back!

Developing a Positive Mental Attitude

Eliminating Negatives

One of the most important principles of the Apex Program is that *success is measured according to whether what you do works.* Your state of mind and how you feel will affect the information you are trying to convey.

Negative/Positive Outcomes

To demonstrate the power of negative and positive outcomes, do the following exercise:

- Find a quiet place where you can concentrate and there are no distractions. If there is a television or radio playing in the background, turn it off.
- Think about an event you do not want to happen, or a situation you would find unpleasant or distasteful. This could involve anything in your life...your career, a personal relationship, a project you're working on, etc.
- Concentrate on it for a few minutes. Put yourself totally in the situation. Hear the sounds, picture the event, and experience the feelings.

In the space below, write down the words that come to mind when you think of the negative outcome from this experience.

Words Associated with Negative Outcome:

- Now think of the same situation, but this time think about it in a positive sense.
- Mentally experience all of the positive aspects. Put yourself totally in the situation. Hear the sounds, picture the event, experience the feelings, etc.
- Think about how great you will feel when you achieve what you want.

In the space below, write down the words that come to mind when you think of the positive outcome from this experience.

Words Associated with Positive Outcome:

When you thought about the two scenarios above, which one did you prefer? The one with the positive outcome, I'm sure! The difference between the two events is not just in your mind, however. If someone had been watching you, they would have noticed a difference in your facial expression, your breathing and your body posture. Physiologically, you become what you think. How you envision your outcome makes a big difference…the difference between success and failure.

Concentrating on what you don't want to happen—sometimes known as worrying—can have a negative impact on more than just your physical body. This has to do with how your brain processes outcomes or desires. Your brain ignores negatives. You may say to yourself, "I don't want to be late for the meeting," but what your brain registers is LATE.

The way to "trick" your brain, if you will, is to tell yourself, "I want to get to the meeting ten minutes early." Your brain hears "early." That's what it records as your desired outcome. It may be difficult at first to eliminate negatives from your thoughts and speech but, with a little practice, it can be done. You'll be amazed at the results.

Eliminating Negative Suggestions

As I just said, your mind works only in positives. When you tell your mind "don't," in order to understand what you "do not" want to happen, your brain must first think about doing the action. Most of us use the "don't" word on a regular basis. We say things like, "Don't forget to pick up bread and milk on the way home." The brain hears, "Forget to pick up bread and milk," and that's what happens. When your brain hears, "Don't be an idiot," or, "Don't pick up that needle," though, the results can be much more disastrous than forgetting a couple of groceries.

Negative Suggestion: Don't think about the cravings for smoking.
Positive Suggestion: Think of breathing clean, fresh air.

Negative Suggestion: Don't think about smoking now.
Positive Suggestion: Keep in mind the reasons you are a smoke-free person, or the feelings you get when you remember that you decided to be smoke-free.

Thought Awareness, Rational Thinking, and Positive Thinking

The three following, related tools are useful in combating negative thinking. Negative thoughts occur when you put yourself down, criticize yourself for errors, doubt your abilities or expect failure. Negative thinking is the negative side of suggestion. Just as making positive statements to yourself helps you to build confidence, develop new habits and improve your mental skills, negative thinking damages these things.

Tool 1: Thought Awareness

Thought awareness is the process by which you observe your thoughts for a time and become aware of the thoughts going through your head. Don't suppress any thoughts… just let them run their course while you observe them.

Watch for negative thoughts while you observe your "stream of consciousness." These will normally appear and disappear without being noticed. Examples of common negative thoughts are:

- Worries about performance
- Preoccupation with the symptoms of stress
- Dwelling on consequences of poor performance
- Self-criticism
- Feelings of inadequacy

Make a note, whether mental or physical, of the thought, and then let the stream of consciousness run on. Thought awareness is the first step in the process of eliminating negative thoughts. After all, you can't counter thoughts you don't know you think!

Rational Thinking

Once you are aware of your negative thoughts, write them down and review them rationally. See whether the thoughts have any basis in reality. Often you'll find that when you challenge negative thoughts, they disappear because you see that they're obviously wrong. They've persisted this long only because they escaped notice.

Positive Thinking and Affirmation

You may find it useful to counter negative thoughts with positive affirmations. You can use affirmations to build confidence and change negative behavior patterns into positive ones. You can base affirmations on clear, rational assessments of fact, and use them to undo the damage that negative thinking may have done to your self-confidence.

Examples of affirmations are:

- I can achieve my goals.
- I am completely myself and people will like me for myself.
- I am completely in control of my life.
- I learn from my mistakes. They increase the basis of experience on which I can draw.
- I am a good, valued person in my own right.
- I am a complete person who functions best breathing clean, smoke-free air.

Not that positive thinking is a magic bullet. Many people have advocated positive thinking almost recklessly, as a solution to everything. As with any tool, you should use it with common sense. Although an Olympic marathon runner is unlikely to have reached that level without being pretty good at positive thinking, no amount of positive thinking will make everyone an Olympic marathon runner! Decide rationally what goals you can realistically attain with hard work, and then use positive thinking to reinforce them.

Remote Brain Control

Need more proof of the awesome power of the brain? John Chapin of the Hahnemann School of Medicine reports in

NatureNeuroscience that they've trained six lab rats to move a robotic arm with the power of thought alone. How did they accomplish that?

First the rats were trained to use their paws to press a spring-loaded lever, which moved a robotic arm that gave them a reward of water or food. This allowed the researchers to discover which brain cells were involved in the task. Once they knew which parts of the brain the rats were using, the researchers implanted electrodes in those areas to study the role of individual neurons. They then had a detailed outline of the neuronal activity that gave rise to the bending, pushing and stretching movements needed to press a lever.

Over many hundreds of trials, the researchers located the neurons responsible for every stage of the action: preparation, flexing the forelimb, extending it, pushing it, and so on. Then the team harnessed those neurons by wiring them so they could fire them directly and move the arm without the animal touching the lever. With this new set-up, the rats quickly learned that there was no need to physically push the lever in order to receive a reward. Within a few tries, they were able to reconfigure their brain activity so that it alone moved the reward-bearing robotic arm.

Putting It Together

If rats can learn to control their brain activity, imagine the possibilities for us! If rats can move a robotic arm using only their minds, can we—as a somewhat higher developed animal—use our conscious thought to direct energy to differently functioning parts of our brains? Could we stimulate growth in the actual structure of the brain itself? Is it possible we could reprogram our subconscious minds to think positive, sober thoughts?

There actually are studies that show that, with conscious attention, you can cause physical changes. This is the basis of biofeedback. There is also some research using MRIs to map brain activity. Again, it seems to be controlled by conscious attention. Once we become aware of how to do it, anything seems possible.

Recent studies show that of you eat a piece of cake, certain neurons light up. If you vividly imagine eating that same cake, the same neurons light up. They're weaker, but they react! Your brain doesn't know the difference between a real and a vividly imagined event.

We know that altered states effect mind/body changes. We can use the skills of NLP and hypnosis to do the same things. This could be our next big breakthrough, using conscious and subconscious thought to alter our physical brains. We could improve our brains with mental exercises the way athletes use physical exercise to alter their bodies. After all, isn't your brain a muscle, a physical organ capable of change and growth?

In the Apex program, I use cutting-edge hypnotic and NLP techniques, based on 25 years of practice and work with thousands of people, to help you do exactly this. My goal is simply to give you the tools I've found and developed, and to show you how to use them for your recovery. Nothing brings me more pleasure than helping another on the path of healing.

I hope to meet you as we trudge this road of recovery together!

Neuro Restructuring Technique: A New Approach

Have you ever noticed that different people react to the same situation much differently? Everyone wants to succeed and be the best that they can be, so what's holding most people back? One person welcomes a challenge with open arms and feels empowered, while another crumbles with the pressure. One person never suffers from an addiction, while another can't function without a "fix." One person can kick a habit after one try, but another continually relapses.

These states of mind are built around your internal representation and physiology, defined by your experiences. Experiences help us form our perception of what is going on around us. The way we embrace new challenges can be changed by how we focus on things and what we focus on. Many people speak a good game. They understand that they must have goals and dreams to achieve the health and freedom they desire. When it actually comes to planning and having the correct goals, though, people often fail miserably.

That's where the Neural Restructuring Technique (NRT) used in the Apex Program is so helpful. NRT treats addictions by strengthening your will to quit, weakening your desire to pursue the subject of the addiction and helping you to concentrate on quitting. It also can be used to focus on the underlying causes of your addiction rather than the addiction itself. This allows you to have the tools you need to overcome your addiction yourself. Now, let's take a look at how NRT does this.

How to Focus Your Brain for Optimum Results

Most people's goals consist only of the things they desire, not true, long-lasting changes. So, you may be wondering, what's the problem with that? It's simple. When your goals are driven only by immediate or short-term desires, you'll be left feeling frustrated and disappointed when they're not achieved. The key to setting goals is to focus on personality changes and behavioral changes. If you change the way you think about your goals, you will succeed. However, if you're only looking for that new BMW or Mercedes, you'll probably be disappointed. Of course, the same is true for addictions. If your goal is to "not be an alcoholic," you may become frustrated. If your goal is to change your behaviors and live the life of someone who doesn't need to drink, your changes will be profound.

When you set goals, you must reach for the stars (which is the easy part), and then be truly committed to what you desire.**FOCUSED ATTENTION IS VITAL!** If you get frustrated because success doesn't fall in your lap, you'll spend the rest of your days chained to your addiction without ever accomplishing your changes. If you really want something, you know you have to continue working until you achieve it. For example, if a person wants to succeed in business, yet is not willing to make the necessary contacts, give countless hours and work hard, how far do you think he or she will get? Not very far. To achieve goals, you have to be able to think outside the box. You have to be willing to work for it and change your thinking. You must be willing to step outside your comfort level and push ahead. Failure is not an option.

Setting Yourself Up For Success

Have you ever heard a story of the extraordinary power or strength of a mother whose child was in danger? Do you know why she was able to achieve that "goal" of protecting her child? It's because, when people's goals are necessities, their thinking changes. When people are required to achieve their goals—when it's "life or death"—they stand up to the pressure and go the extra mile to ensure they complete the correct actions. This is because there's a sense of urgency and need. This is great news for any addict, because it allows us to see that we can control our motivation and the programming of our minds.

You must set yourself up for success. Your motivation lies in your "self talk" and the words that you feed yourself every day. The excuses and "I'll do it tomorrows" have to cease. You need to have a sense of urgency in completing your goal. If someone held a gun to your loved-one's head and told you that he would kill your loved one if you didn't put down the cigarettes or booze or food, wouldn't you stop that behavior? You bet! When the stakes are raised, you require more of yourself. You're also giving yourself positive feedback, because you're telling yourself you must achieve...or else. You're reading this because, on some level, you realize that really is the case with your addiction. You have to achieve freedom from your behavior...or else. Now you have to make that realization a driving force in achieving your goal.

There are very few individuals in this world who are incapable of achieving their goals. When it becomes a "must" to succeed, people pull out all the stops and jump all the hurdles. The best way to accomplish this with your own goal is to raise the stakes and give yourself the credit you deserve.

Don't sell yourself short. When people do that, they fail. When you give yourself negative feedback, you give up because you feel you simply can't meet the expectations of the goal. This is where frustration comes in and makes you give up and look for a new goal...like finding that next hit. If you don't want to fail, your "should" goal needs to become a "must."

Think About Your Past Achievements

Think back to the goals you've achieved in your life. What was your mindset? Why was your goal achieved? Did you give up along the way? There probably was a point in time when you thought about throwing in the towel, but didn't. For some reason, your goal was a "must" to you. It may have been a job, money or something as basic as learning to play an instrument, but you achieved it.

When it came time to file your taxes, did you get it done? Yes, because you knew if you didn't, you'd have to answer to the taxman. (That, or you're answering to the IRS right now!) Think about your education. You knew if you didn't finish, you'd spend the rest of your days making minimum wage or, worse, digging a ditch. It was a requirement, a "must", and you knew that, no matter what the obstacle, you must overcome it. It's no different with addiction, or any other goal you set in life. You must tell yourself you have no choice. There's no room for quitting, or for "tomorrow." It must be done today.

Take a few minutes and think of three things you want to accomplish but have been putting off. Be honest with yourself. Don't give yourself any slack or start making excuses...that's the reason you haven't succeeded before today. List these three things, and then we'll look at how to get the ball rolling.

1.
2.
3.

Raise the Bar on Your Acceptance Level

When we dream, we generally dream big. We dream of things like becoming president, or owning a multi-million dollar home or a high-end sports car. When we set our goals, though, we settle. Sure, we'd like to make $10,000 a month, but we're willing to settle for $3,000 per month. We sell ourselves short, every time. Why is this?

If you settle, then you don't reach for any other expectations. Worse, you'll be left settling for the rest of your life. On the other hand, if you're satisfied with $3,000 per month, but continue on to strive for $10,000 per month, you'll achieve that higher amount. People gravitate to their goals, especially when they feel they must.

Think about it this way. When you're short on cash for the month, and the bills haven't been paid and the cabinets are bare, you pull some overtime or take a second job. You know you must achieve another $500 dollars, or your family will go hungry and your electricity will be shut off. That's not an acceptable option. So, regardless of how tired or worn out you are, you continue on to achieve that goal. That's because you've raised your expectation level and are telling yourself you can't settle for what you have today.

Change Your Language

Give up words such as "should," "would," "could" and "if." They can no longer be a part of your goal or dreams. "I wish" becomes "I will." It may sound trivial or silly, but it truly works. Look at people like Donald Trump, Oprah, the President and others who have achieved the ultimate success in their lives. Listen to their words. Do they say, "I wish I could have"? NO! They speak as if everything is a work in progress, because it is. They continually reach for higher standards and dreams. They don't sell themselves short; they don't settle.

You must foster your creativity, be good to yourself and allow yourself to grow. If you don't grow as a person, your dreams and goals will go right out the window. Positive self-esteem, a positive identity, is one of the most important factors in achieving success. So, instead of telling yourself you'll do it tomorrow, tell yourself you'll complete it today. No more settling for excuses. There is no choice; it has become a must. "Could have," "would have" and "should have" are gone from your vocabulary.

You have to start using "must" language with your internal dialog. You'll respond more to those things that you "MUST" do. If you raise the bar on your inner dialog, it will bring it to new levels. I also suggest you adopt the phrase, "Failure is not an option." When Cortez landed in the New World, he burned the boats, so his men knew that they *could not* fail. Try that inner attitude on for a change!

Focusing Attention in a Situation

Sometimes, though, it's difficult to focus on your goal. There are millions of stimuli thrown at your brain in any one second. The brain acts like a filter and sorts through these stimuli, determining what needs attention. The brain does this, in part, through an information process known as "chunking."

Chunking is basically the ability to group certain memories together for ready recall. For example, the memory of a high-school play may be associated with the musty-smelling cologne of a history teacher and the way that teacher twirled his mustache. Obviously, there were several other behaviors, actions and environments happening at the same time, but those are the pieces your brain chunked together.

Now think about the memories associated with a point of failure in your life. Most people recall this information and replay the "failing" moments over and over again. Instead of turning this information into feedback, and learning from it, they begin to feed negative thoughts into their heads. How successful do you think this makes the person? Not very! In fact, it sets them up for failure. The question then becomes, "How do I change this state and look at my experiences in a positive light?"

The answer is, *change the way you focus on things.* Instead of always picking up on the negative, or how you screwed up, turn it around and replay the situation with a more positive note. Imagine that the "screw up" was resolved. See yourself succeeding. When you do this, you're changing how you focus.

After the years of a negative internal script, your brain goes on autopilot and focuses on the negative in every situation. This will take a little bit to change; your internal scripting has to become positive just as it first became negative. You'll have to remain constant in redirecting your focus to the positive, but stay with it. After a while, your mind will change to a positive autopilot mode. Yes, it takes work, but it can be done.

Directing Your Focus

Our internal scripting is based on not only what we think, but also how we feel. It's possible to create a mental image to motivate and draw focus to a particular scenario. As we've already found, the intensity of a state of mind is based on the intensity of the situation or the picture you have of that situation.

That all sounds confusing, but here's an example: most people feel motivated to go shopping. Sometimes, though, the motivation is more intense than at other times, right? This is because of our mental images about the situation. Shopping may not be as much fun when there are issues such as money, time or finding the right piece of clothing. On the other hand, imagine yourself winning a $50,000 shopping spree for anything you want. Does that change the scenario? Of course it does. It's a bigger, clearer and brighter picture in your mind.

That's how visualization can change your state of mind just by changing the intensity of the pictures in your mind. Your mind is drawn to a bigger, more distinct set of pictures. What do I mean by more intense pictures? Think about it. The colors, sounds, light and angles all add to the intensity and desire of a movie. If the picture is small, colors are dim and the angle is off, would it be as interesting? NO!

The pictures in our minds oftentimes are automatic, leaving us with little control. This, however, can be changed. The way to fix this is to focus on positive pictures and images of success. Make a mental "movie" of those pictures. Eventually, the mind will begin automatically playing more positive images.

Submodalities: The Keys to the Brain

The brain is often referred to as a large operating computer. The submodalities, or "keys," to the mind allow you to control actions, thoughts and perceptions. These submodalities are put into three categories: visual (sight), auditory (sound) and kinesthetic (feeling). Let's look at the three submodalities and their input. In order to understand our state of mind, we must understand our brain's coding system.

The **visual** submodalities are how your brain codes pictures or sights. Think about looking at a picture. The things you notice in a picture are what your brain is coding about what you're physically seeing. Is the picture focused or out of focus? What is the location of the item in the picture? Is it framed or panoramic? Is it disassociated or associated?

The **auditory** submodalities are the way your brain codes sounds. Is it loud or soft, slow or fast, in tune or out of tune?

Kinesthetic submodalities are the brain's coding of internal feelings. This is one of the more difficult coding systems to understand, because it's not always as clear-cut as the others. The location of the feeling, whether it's still or moving, if it's light or heavy, and the direction of movement are all taken into consideration in the coding process.

Coding and internal scripting is different for everyone. Finding the way your brain codes and creates a particular situation is a discovery process. It's also a very important step toward success in breaking free of your addiction.

Disassociation & Association

There are two types of image coding of the brain; disassociation and association. When you visualize a past event or situation in your life, do you see yourself at a distance or through your own eyes? If you're seeing the situation from a distance, this is disassociation. When you visualize the event from your own eyes, this is association. We tend to visualize negative events from a distance, or as a disassociation, and positive events with association. The association or disassociation can have a great impact on one's state of mind. Here's why:

Close your eyes and remember back to a positive event in your life. Remember the location, smells, sounds and who is there with you. Visualize the situation through your own eyes and walk through the experience in your mind. This inspires a good and positive feeling. Now, take that same situation and visualize it from a distance (disassociation). You're basically stepping out of your body and removing yourself from the events. Do you see how your mood and state of mind changes? It has a great impact, because the more involved we are with a positive feeling, the better state we will be in.

Ability to Intensify Any State

Wouldn't it be great to be able to intensify or replicate a feeling or state on cue? It would be like having a magic wand. Unfortunately, no one has developed this wand, so we have to come up with another way to intensify a positive state. Intensifying involves shifting the submodalities. Here's how:

- Imagine and visualize a goal that you want to achieve, but have not found the motivation to achieve.
- Close your eyes and visualize yourself achieving that goal.
- Take notes about all the submodalities involved in the experience. Make mental notes of whether the situation is disassociated or associated. Note the

sights, sounds and the shape of the feelings (light or heavy, or whether there is movement).

- Rate the submodalities on a scale of 1-10, with ten being the highest amount of motivation and intensity you felt as you stood in achievement of your goal.

Mapping Across Love to Disgust

You can also feel differently about a situation. It's just a matter of shifting your submodalities. There are steps you can take to change motivation to un-motivation, or turn love to disgust. Of course, it's great to be able to change an unmotivated goal to a motivated goal, but the reverse is sometimes necessary, as well. Think about when you are motivated toward that bowl of ice cream…a whopping 500 calories. In order to break your food addiction and achieve your dream weight, you must become unmotivated quickly. With that in mind, here are the five steps to control motivation:

Step One: Elicit the submodalities of a food you love

Imagine a food that is not the healthiest choice, but that's one you really want. Perhaps it's a big, juicy steak. Whatever the food, make mental notes about the submodalities. (Because this food is a substance, most of the submodalities will involve kinesthetics.) Imagine the smell, feel and, most of all, the taste. On a scale of 1-10, rate all the things you like about this type of food. (Since you like this food, most of them should be up toward 10.)

Step Two: Elicit the submodalities of a food you hate

Now think of a food that you don't like at all. Deviled eggs, perhaps. Imagine eating it. Imagine the smell and the taste. Think of how it makes you feel. Imagine what you would feel like chewing and swallowing the food. Are you feeling sick? Probably. Now, take note of all the submodalities involved in disliking this food.

Step Three: The difference between the liked and disliked foods

There are some definite differences here, as there should be. One food you like, and the other you despise. The differences between the two are called *drivers.* The steak is hot. Deviled eggs are cold. The steak smells good. Deviled eggs smell nasty. Steak is dark and pleasing to the eye, while the deviled eggs are pale and pasty.

Step Four: Replacing the likes with dislikes

Now, imagine that hot and juicy steak, but replace it with those deviled eggs. Imagine yourself eating the steak, but imagine that it tastes and feels like those deviled eggs that you absolutely hate. Imagine how they taste and what they feel like going down. Separate yourself from that steak by stepping out and making the visual smaller. How badly do you want that steak now?

Step Five: Test it

Granted, you wouldn't always want to replace steak and never eat it again, but this kind of replacement can be used as a tool to control intensity and state of mind. We've used food in this example, but this replacement method is a great way to neutralize any type of craving or compulsion. It can help you turn off those obsessions for things you don't need or that are bad for you.

These are a few of the ways the Neural Reprogramming Technique can help you overcome addictions and reach your goals. That's not the whole story, though. Next, we'll take a look at how your brain and its programming affect your behavior.

Human Hardware

Throughout history, people have puzzled over the question, "Why are some people more successful than others?" While the explanation includes the relationship between genes, physical environment, socioeconomics and cultural indicators, the simple explanation involves *programming*.

In the early 1970s, a team of scientists at the University of California at Santa Cruz set out to answer the question of why people with similar backgrounds in education, training, and experience were not similarly successful. They wanted to explore what they called "the secrets of effective people" and wanted to "model human excellence." They discovered that, while backgrounds were similar, the brain wiring—or programming—was distinctly different. Out of this research developed the field of neurolinguistic programming (NLP). The phrase "neurolinguistic programming" is actually a combination of three words:

- neuro: referring to the brain
- linguistic: referring to verbal and non-verbal content
- programming: manipulation of content

NLP rests on the premise that thought patterns (programming) are largely responsible for an individual's success or failure. This means that preconceived thoughts and mental conditioning effect the way interact with others and your accomplishments. The theory is that if you "remodel" your negative thoughts, you can change your personal situation. This remodeling of thoughts requires a process called *neurogenesis*. We'll talk about neurogenesis in a little while. First, though, let's look at some more ways you brain is programmed.

Meta Programs

In NLP, we talk about how people use strategies to make decisions or create beliefs. These strategies aren't conscious; far from it. They are strategies you use at the unconscious level. Even people who use the same strategies, though, may arrive at very different conclusions. For instance, one person may mentally picture several options and choose one that feels right, while another may mentally picture the same options but feel overwhelmed by the sheer number of choices, and be unable to choose at all. What causes this?

Differences like these are caused by Meta Programs. The word "meta" simply means "outside of," so Meta Programs are mental programs *outside of* your decision-making strategies. You can think of Meta Programs as habits of thought. They're the processes we use every day to filter what we pay attention to from what we ignore. While your conscious mind can only pay attention to about seven (give or take a couple) things at once, your senses are bombarded by millions of perceptions every second. You need some way to filter through all that input and decide what needs your attention. That's where your Meta Programs come in.

Sometimes, as with addiction, the Meta Program we use isn't necessarily the best one for the situation. That was really bad a couple of decades ago, when scientists still thought you were stuck with the Meta Programs you had. Fortunately, research by Robert Dilts showed that Meta Programs could be changed or replaced through the use of NLP.

Please don't think I mean that some Meta Programs are good and some are bad. All of them can be either good or bad; it's depends on where and when you use them. In fact, you may use one Meta Program in one situation and another under different circumstances. Most of us lean toward certain programs, though. It's helpful to know which programs you're using, and how they affect you. Once you know what lies underneath your thought processes, you have the freedom to change the way you operate.

With that in mind, let's look at a few of the Meta Programs.

Toward vs. Away-From

In this program, you're either focused on getting what you want, or not getting what you don't want.

It's common for people with problems to use the away-from program and express themselves in terms of what they don't want. Unfortunately, they sometimes focus so much on what they *don't* want that they don't know what they *do* want. Not only do they not know what they want, but they don't even perceive anything they want. It's like it's not even there. When you constantly focus on what you don't want, you may end up believing that something you might want doesn't even exists. Another downside is that away-from thinking constantly draws your attention to negatives, because if you can't see the negatives, you can't get away from them! Because energy follows attention, you'll likely end up seeing, remembering and even attracting more negative experiences.

It also creates problems in goal-setting. If you're moving away from something (i.e., I don't want to be a drug addict), you may never know when you reach your goal… or you may relapse into having the same goal once again.

Not that away-from Meta Programs are all bad. In certain contexts, they are more useful that toward programs. For instance, soldiers during combat missions might have a priority of "Don't shoot our own guys." This is away-from thinking, but it avoids many "friendly fire" tragedies.

As a default program, though, toward thinking is much better at creating a healthy, happy life. That's probably why Western society usually rewards people who have toward thinking. It's certainly the better choice for setting goals. Imagine the differences in these two goals:

I *don't want* to smoke cigarettes. (Away-From thinking.)

I *want* to breathe clean air and improve my health so I can dance at my granddaughter's wedding. (Toward thinking.)

As I said before, though, all Meta Programs can have downsides. For instance, toward thinking can lead you to make unwise or risky decisions without thinking about the potential dangers to be avoided. You may even have been using toward thinking when you first pursued the drug or behavior to which you're now addicted...you moved toward the illusion of relief without thinking of the pitfalls of addiction, broken relationships and lost opportunities.

Best-Case vs. Worst-Case Scenario

When you use this Meta Program, you're either focused on the possibilities of a situation or on the problems. Generally, seeing the best-case scenario is a more optimistic way of seeing the world, while worst-case thinking puts you in a negative frame of mind.

Putting it that way might make best-case scenario thinking seem the better of the two, but that's not necessarily true. When you realistically examine the worst possible case and plan for it, anything else that happens seems easy by comparison. If you use best-case thinking all the time, without exception, you could be naïve to risk, possibly trusting people who shouldn't be trusted.

That said, though, many people have problems with consistent worst-case thinking in their lives. If you constantly use worst-case thinking, you may be unable to envision any kind of positive outcome for yourself. You may get stuck in a self-reinforcing loop that leads to panic or depression. Even if you realize that your thinking doesn't make much sense, without the means to change it, you're stuck in your worst possible situation. Here are a couple of examples of extreme best-case and worst-case thinking:

Now that I've joined A.A., it'll be easy. I'll kick the habit and never relapse again! (Best-Case Scenario thinking.)

I want a drink, so I'm probably going to give in. If I give in, I'll go on a binge and relapse. If I relapse, I might as well give up...I'll never quit. (Worst-Case Scenario thinking.)

Many successful and happy people find that the best use of this Meta Program lies in the middle. Think of it like, "Expect the best, plan for the worst."

Big Chunk vs. Little Chunk

When you use big chunk thinking, you see the "big picture." It's helpful for envisioning, getting perspective and setting direction. Little chunk thinking sees the details. It's useful for putting a plan into action and making progress in manageable steps.

Like all Meta Programs, both sides have their place. How can you set goals if you can't envision the bigger outcome?

On the other hand, how can you reach your goal without seeing the steps you need to take to get there?

I'm going to kick this drug habit, mend my relationships and have a successful business. (Big Chunk thinking.)

I'm going to follow the 12 steps of Narcotics Anonymous to become clean and sober. (Little Chunk thinking.)

Each of those goals is good in its own way, but you really need both—the vision and the plan—to successfully break you addiction. Big chunk thinking leads you astray when you dream ineffectively, but little chunk thinking can lead you to obsess and not be able to "see the forest for the trees." Each is helpful, but only in the right context.

There are many more Meta Programs under which you operate every day. (Experts count between 50 and 60.) Others include Self Reference vs. Other Reference, Association vs. Disassociation, Match vs. Mismatch, and Proactive vs. Reactive. Knowing the programs is only part of the puzzle. Once you know which Meta Programs you use, and how they help you or hold you back, you need to know how to change them.

Imagine the freedom of being able to recognize how your brain is operating against you and being able to train it, like a computer, to run a whole new "program." That's part of what I cover in the Apex Program. Through the NLP tools I give you, you will be able to step into a new way of operating at will. Your actions will become a matter of choice, not rote programming. With that flexibility, you'll discover new resources within yourself...resources you never knew you had.

Neurogenesis

Simply described, neurogenesis is the creation of new nerve connections in the brain. These nerve connections are kind of like the hardwiring of a computer. However, while the computer relies on hardware composed of digital circuitry, the human brain relies on hardware composed of neural circuitry made up of billions of neurons (nerve cells) forming a complex neurological system (nervous system). These neurons assess your environment and react to your environment by sending chemical messages to each other through electrical impulses. As we talked about in the chapter on obsession and compulsion, these messages form the basis of our learning, productivity, behavior and even our survival.

Neurogenesis is essential to success in humans. Since we often look to scientific studies of other species to explain behavior in humans, let me share a fascinating study about canaries. Frederick Nottebohm's studies, performed in the early 1990s, illustrate the importance of neurogenesis in songbirds. The songbird depends on its beautiful melodies to attract a mate and produce offspring, ensuring its lineage.

In his studies, Nottenbohm discovered that, in order to sing these complex melodies, the male birds continually generated new brain cells in their song center. In fact, approximately one percent of their neurons are created in the song center daily. Because human behavior is so individually varied, we can't assess the daily potential of new neural connections. If you compare the canary brain capacity to that of a human, though, you can imagine the possibilities!

You've probably heard the statement that humans use only 10% of their brains. This isn't exactly true. It's more correct to say that humans use only 10% of their neurons at any one time. This means that the more new neural connections you build, the greater productivity you can expect from your active 10%. What great news about your potential!

The Brain as a Computer

Before, we compared the brain's neural circuitry to the hardwiring of a computer. Let's take a closer look at this comparison. Both the computer and the human brain have massive information-processing abilities that are based on the transmission of electrical signals. Both have a memory that can grow and learn to accommodate changing needs. However, both can also be damaged by faulty programming information. For a computer this faulty information comes in the form of viruses. In the human brain, this faulty information is negativity. Fortunately, both systems can be repaired.

There is a fundamental difference between computer hardware and the human neurological system, though. While computing hardware may vastly vary from computer to computer, every person possesses the same neural hardware. We all share a basic physical neurology with billions of neurons processing approximately 40,000 bits of information per second. All those neurons aid the brain in reasoning, learning, and memory. In the absence of a disease, or physical damage or defect, we all possess the same neural hardware. Read that again: *every human being shares the same neural hardware.* So, if we all share the same hardware, then we all share the same potential!

If we all have the same potential shouldn't we all be equally successful? This is where programming comes in.

Programming is the underlying answer to why some people are more successful than others. Most of us have heard the old axiom, "It is not what you have, but how you use it." This rings true when it comes to brain neurology. The actual wiring of your brain—the number of neural connections—depends on your individual programming. Too often, mental resources are not used to their full potential, and the wiring is damaged through faulty programming. Chemical abuse can also damage the wiring. Proper programming involves positive, nurturing input.

Until the last decade, the prevailing scientific theory of neurology was that the human brain couldn't establish new neural connections. In other words, we thought that what you are born with is what you have and, as you age, they will die. We now know that the more than one hundred billion neurons of your brain are geared to reinvest in themselves. Positive, enriched environments stimulate your brain to create more neural connections. The more you learn, the more you become capable of learning. You can actually rewire, or reprogram, your brain! What's more, you can do this at any age. The more you stimulate your brain, the more it grows!

Negative Programming

While positive programming stimulates neurogenesis, negative programming stops it. Negative programming includes any feedback that acts as a stressor. A stressor, whether internal or external, produces a biochemical stress response.

The stress response process was first described by Hans Selye in the 1930s. Selye described it as "the rate of wear and tear on the body." Broadly, the term "stress response" describes the biochemical reaction to a threat to a person's biological balance (also known as homeostasis). While researchers agree on the physiological and psychological effects of stress on the human body, the term itself remains somewhat of an abstract concept because it's dependent on human perception. In other words, the occurrence of stressors (things that cause stress), as well as the degree of stress response, depends on individual analysis of the situation. This is actually a good thing, because it means it's not set in stone. It can be altered!

Stressors can be either external (coming from someone else) or internal (coming from yourself). Stressors also fall into categories of:

- positive or negative
- acute or chronic (ongoing)
- mental or physical

From these categories, many combinations can occur. Not all are bad. Acute stress is actually helpful, temporarily flooding the body with hormones to assist in regaining homeostasis. For example, positive-acute-mental stress could be exemplified by the exuberance of winning a Nobel Prize. Certainly, no one could call this a bad thing, but the body still gets a little overwhelmed and needs to regain balance! Alternatively, chronic stress is damaging, continually flooding the body with hormones. Over time, those constantly active hormones can damage mental functions. As an example, negative-chronic-mental stress could come in the form of everyday worries such as low self-esteem. Low self-esteem is an example of negative programming. It also becomes self-reinforcing.

Regardless of the source, the effect of continued stress from negative programming is toxic. This means that, when the brain is constantly exposed to worry and negativity, homeostasis (balance) becomes the priority and all other neural functioning suffers. In this situation, existing neurons are preoccupied with survival and the brain does not exert effort on creating new neurons.

Elizabeth Gould's studies have documented this chronic stress effect in primates. These studies show that when a primate is under chronic stress, "Its brain begins to starve. It stops creating new cells. The cells it already has retreat inwards. The mind is disfigured." If that's the case in primates, imagine the effect of chronic stress—low self-esteem, financial worries, or battling an addiction—in your own life.

Broken Windows Theory

"Broken Windows" is a social theory relating to urban vandalism. The theory states that if windows in an abandoned building are broken and then left unrepaired, the community will believe such vandalism is acceptable. Further, if let go, the vandalism will spread into other parts of the community. Immediate repair of the broken windows and steps to prevent future incidents, though, sends the message that vandalism is not acceptable and will not be tolerated. The same theory has been expanded to graffiti, resulting in the push to "clean up the environment" in inner cities.

This same theory could be applied to negative programming of the human brain. If the brain is exposed to negative programming without intervention, the individual will believe this is acceptable. Failure, if accepted, becomes the norm. Any such negative programming, if left unaddressed, will develop into chronic mental stress. This affects the structure of the brain and reduces your potential to be successful. However, introduction of positive programming will rewire your brain, producing new neural connections and increasing your individual success potential. Talk about great news!

Levels of Change

Perspective Is Everything!

Perspective is basically how you feel and think about things that happen to you. That's a small statement, but it says big things about a person's ability to change or break an addiction.

Sometimes your perspective on new experiences, tasks or information can guide you in the wrong direction, so it's important to learn to control your thinking. When you control your thinking, you can handle change in smaller steps, making the change more manageable. Smaller and more manageable steps make the change seem easier. That creates more confidence and allows you to better handle the situation.

Another way to look at it is to think of your brain as a big information system, kind of like a series of maps. These maps grow as you receive new information and experiences into your system. There's a lot of territory around these maps in our brains, and sometimes our perspective restrains the incoming information, therefore limiting our maps.

Logical Levels

There are different levels at which change can occur. As with anything, it's easier to change things at a lower level than at a higher level.

For example, when you think of remodeling your home, you think of colors, decorations and minor repairs. These are all steps that are easy, even fun (and which won't cost an arm and leg!). The higher level remodeling jobs, such as electrical, plumbing and replacing the carpet, are much more difficult. Well, the same holds true when you begin to remodel your life.

The different levels of change involve environment, behaviors, skills, beliefs, identity and purpose. We might also add spirituality, since faith is an important step in many successful 12-step programs.

When you begin to rid yourself of an addiction or habit, you need to examine the levels and determine the level of change you're looking for. When all the levels are satisfied, you'll find you're happier and more content. This can be called *congruence*, which is the state of an individual when they're comfortable with their values and skills. Misalignment, or levels that are out of order, can cause your thought patterns to work against you, leading to failure.

The Right Questions

When you want to make any change, it's important to have a good foundation. You need to understand why you're changing. Many people are amazed that, even with an addiction, answering *why* is sometimes the hardest part. Plus, to be successful in breaking your addiction, you also need to answer *who, what, where, when* and *how*.

To help you with those answers, here are some questions you need to ask yourself in order to determine the best plan of action, and to know if the change is a good one.

First, the **environment** surrounding your change is very important. Your environment is sometimes the factor that constrains change in your life. Some people are confined to the environment in which they live. Sometimes you can change your environment, and other times you have to find a way to change in spite of it. The environment can answer your *where, when* and *who* questions...in what place do you need to change, when are the events or circumstances that you need to change, and who needs to be present—or not—for you to change?

Second, **behavior** involves the actions and behaviors surrounding your changes. This is the *what* question. After all, the behavior is what you need to change. Behavior is also directly linked to the environment level.

Third, **capabilities** involve your knowledge base. *How* can you accomplish your change using your skills? Your capabilities are your guiding force.

Fourth, **beliefs** and values are your motivational base. They're what allow you to begin the change itself. Why do you want to get rid of this addiction? This, obviously, is your *why* question. It shows the importance you place on the change.

Fifith, **identity** is your sense of self. In many cases, it also shows your relation to others. This is the *who* question. Who are you? Who are you to yourself? Who are you to others?

Purpose, rather than being a level all to itself, means looking at the big picture. This is sometimes difficult. Purpose is the driving force behind the change, as well as the reason why it is necessary. You can think of purpose as the *what for* question. What am I changing for?

Logical Levels Step-by-Step

One of the areas where most people go wrong is in not establishing a guideline, a so-called "method to their madness." Using the levels and breaking your change into smaller steps will ensure your success.

Think about it this way; when a person goes to climb a mountain, the climber doesn't take one huge step in hopes of reaching the top. That would be ridiculous! They take a series of carefully-planned, smaller steps to get there. The same is true for achieving any goal, even overcoming addiction. Develop a plan and take smaller steps!

Out of Whack

The old saying that you cannot fix what you do not acknowledge is very true. It's important to admit that a change is necessary. Whatever change it may be, whatever it may be worth to you, if you don't put a price tag on it, you probably won't follow the steps!

The Right Level

After admitting there's a need for change, you must discover at what level the change is needed. Taking inventory will help you discover the level of change that is needed. For example, what area in your life is suffering? Is it personal, business or another area? How could it improve?

Putting It into Action

As with any change in your life, leaving behind an addiction must come from motivation and from an understanding that a change will help you succeed or better your life. It's also necessary to find the right tools to help you succeed. Those tools may be other people, education, business or something else that provides the needed foundation for your change.

Uses for Logical Levels

Using logical levels can assist you in springing into action after you've answered all the questions and surrounded yourself with useful tools. Here's how to use the levels in a practical and efficient manner:

Information Gathering

Getting the facts and making use of them is very important. You wouldn't do a research paper without first gathering the information. After finding the information, organize it into a system you can understand.

Building Relationships

Building relationships within your family is important in any change, because it typically changes the dynamics of the entire family. This is especially true with a substance-abuse problem, where the entire family is probably affected. Understanding how the family can work together and using family bonds will help you continue and will make your change more successful.

Improve Performance

Addiction is a personal problem, but it spills over into your business and other aspects of your life. Whatever is affected, though, it's important to ensure that you're doing your best. You may need to decide at what level, or where, the change is necessary. Do you need to perform better at work, or is it your friendships that are suffering?

Leadership and Confidence

Finally, using the levels of change is important to establish better confidence levels. Without confidence in yourself, your methods and your goals, you are more likely to relapse into old addictions and behaviors. Confidence allows you to stay on track and create the change you desire.

Finding the Tools for Change

There are certain requirements that are needed for change. Among those requirements are the desire to change, knowing how to change and the opportunity for change. Deciding that you can make it happen, and accepting the fact that you have choices, will assist you in the change process.

Now that we've taken a brief look at the levels, and how you can use them to overcome addiction, let's go a little deeper.

Environment

Your surroundings are one of the most important aspects of change. Environment is everywhere. You are physically present wherever you live, work or play. To recover from your addiction, you must get your environment to support you in your effort to become a new person.

Sometimes the environment is simply not conducive to change, so change becomes impossible. Instead of giving up hope, try changing your environment to a more encouraging surrounding. This will make it easier for you to achieve your goal. To put it bluntly, you don't go to a whore house to listen to a piano player! You also don't have to go to a bar (or a Dairy Queen or a drug dealer) to cash your check. You're learning the language of addiction-free living, so you need to surround yourself with others who speak that new language.

Here are a few environmental questions to help decide the right environment choices for you:

- In what circumstances do I least feel the need to use?
- What surroundings best help me avoid the substance or behavior?
- What time of day do I have the least desire to use?

Behavior

Yes, the behavior is what must change. Changing your behavior, though, is about more than not drinking or smoking or getting high. What about the behavior of having fun? Can you have fun sober, party without getting high, celebrate without gorging yourself, or relax without a cigarette? If you can't, then you need to get new behaviors

When we talk about Neuro Restructuring Technique, we talk about behavior as not only your observable actions, but also the way you feel about your actions. How you feel about your behavior is generally the driving force behind the action. It's what inspires the action again and again. That feeling may well be the purpose that drives your behavior. Until you understand that, you may have a difficult time changing your actions.

Determining whether or not your behavior is in line with your goals is sometimes difficult, but here are a few questions that can help.

- Is your behavior consistent with your goals?
- Are your behaviors positive, and do they keep you happy?
- Is there a pattern in your behavior? If so, is it consistent with your goals?
- How do other people react to your behaviors? Are there patterns?
- Does your body language change in different situations? If so, note the differences.

Maximizing positive behavior is important when on the path toward addiction-free living. That's true whether it means having a salad at dinner or going jogging when you feel stressed. At first, it's a conscious effort to maximize the right behaviors, but after a while it becomes old hat. On the flip side, you'll want to decrease bad behaviors until you eliminate them.

Skills/Capabilities

Because the human mind is a learning machine, there's no doubt that some people have inborn skills or talents. Some people seem more "capable" than others. Oftentimes, others mistakenly think it is based on intelligence or, in the case of addictions, moral superiority. That's simply not the case. Researchers now know that the best employees, for instance, are those who are team-oriented and who have a positive attitude. Those who approach change with a positive spirit can acquire new skills and capabilities.

When it comes to addiction, that's exactly what you need...new skills. You need the skill to relax without alcohol or a cigarette or marijuana, to get motivated without speed or chocolate or the chance to place a bet. You need the skills of the new person you want to be.

Just like you learn to ride a bike or ski, you can learn new things, if you have the desire and right attitude. One of the core ideas of Apex is the fact that all skills are learnable. You can learn healthy living by watching, and modeling your behavior on, those who live healthy lives.

Asking yourself the following questions can help you get an idea of your capabilities and help you better understand where you can make improvements.

- What skill or skills have you learned previously?
- What events, happenings and situations led to the positive learning of that skill? What pattern do you see that can help you make it happen again?

- What you are good at? What do others compliment you on?

Recognizing the patters and behaviors around these questions can help you focus your attention on your ability to learn new skills. That ability will lead to your success in living without the drug or behavior that has held you back.

Beliefs

Beliefs and values drive people to either achieve their goals or be lost in trying. The way you feel about something, especially your goal, motivates you to continue on.

Do your beliefs support the new you? If you were raised in an alcoholic family, they might not. You might have been raised to believe that "Real men drink," "Real men can hold their booze," "You can't have fun without drinking," or "I need to relax after work with a drink." Where food is an issue, the refrain is, "Eat something, you'll feel better" or "Clean your plate, kids are starving in Africa." When these are your beliefs, the question becomes, *do you believe you can change?* Is change easy or hard?

Seeking out a goal is not always easy. Since success doesn't come overnight, though, motivation is imperative. Our beliefs not only keep us moving toward the end result, but also help us rank our goals and wants. If you have two important things on your agenda, you have to rank them and make a decision as to which comes first. Most people will move toward the goal, or "thing," that has the highest price tag. For example, we may get great recognition for playing a round of golf, but if we fail to go to work, the money is shut off. You may get a great buzz from that third beer, but if you come home drunk again, your spouse may leave you. Which action carries the greatest value?

Beliefs also keep you in the place or environment where you need to be. If your goal is to get into shape, then your goal is best achieved in a gym or other fitness area. You believe that fitness is associated with the gym, not the ice-cream parlor. Controlling your obsession with chocolate is best served at a salad bar, not a candy store.

Our beliefs and values drive the lower logical levels, allowing all the levels to come into alignment. If you're concerned that there may be a conflict between the levels, here are some questions to help you make a determination.

- What is important to you, and why?
- What is important to others?
- What do you believe to be the difference between right and wrong?

Identity

Is partying part of who you are? Are you a Marlborough man, or a Bud man? If that is your identity, then you have to change who you are. The same person continues the same action, picks up the same drink, and takes the same drug.

Many people think a person's identity is based on his or her skills, intelligence and behavior. In the Apex Program, we look at the identity of the person as separate from behavior. Instead of lumping people into a category based on their actions, behavior is a consequence of an underlying motive. This belief is an optimistic view of mankind, and avoids attaching labels to people based on their behavior.

This may not sound like a major theory, but it is. The way we speak to others says a great deal about our expectations of them. If we speak to someone about bad behavior, and attach it to their identity—as when we call someone a drunk, a druggie, or even a smoker—we're sending them the message that their character is flawed. That's why it's important to speak about the behavior and avoid negative comments about the person's identity, *even when we're speaking about ourselves.*

Here are some questions for you to answer if there's conflict surrounding identity:

- How do you express yourself?
- How do you feel about yourself?
- How do others feel about you?
- Do you label others?
- Do others have an accurate picture of who you really are?

Purpose

Purpose is generally the reason why people journey onward toward their goal. Some people journey through life questioning their purpose in life, even though it's right in front of them. They're looking too hard!

For others, their purpose is larger than their identity, and they achieve great things. Through hard times and great suffering, there have been individuals who have persevered because their passion was greater than any other thing in their life. Look at the Dalai Lama and the resistance and suffering he endured. His passion was definitely a driving force. Some might say his passion was the *only* force.

A passion for something will generally keep an individual on track for much longer than normal. People will endure great things when they feel strongly about something. Finding a passion or purpose will guide you toward your goal regardless of the conflict or troubles you cross during your journey. Answering the following questions will help with your purpose.

- Why are you here on earth?
- How do you want people to remember you when you die?
- What strengths can you use to contribute to a higher good?

Spiritual

Spirituality also plays an important role in the lives of many. If that's the case for you, ask yourself these questions:

- Does your idea of a higher power support the new you?
- If God is with you, who can be against you?

Recognizing Your Logical Levels

So, how do you know which of your levels needs to change for you to break free from your addiction?

By examining your thoughts and comments, you can determine your levels of conflict. Being able to determine your level will let you make the necessary changes. When you look at your own statements, you need to realize that it's not always what you say, but where you place the emphasis in the sentence. Here are some statements and evaluations:

I can't do it here.	Statement about *identity*.
I *can't* do it here.	Statement about *beliefs*.
I can't *do* it here.	Statement about *capability*.
I can't do *it* here.	Statement about *behavior*.
I can't do it *here*.	Statement about *environment*.

Triggers

I'm sure there have been times in your life when you've enjoyed a positive state of mind. You probably also understand what it feels like to be in a negative state of mind. Given the chance, most people would choose the positive state of mind, but most feel their attitude is simply based on environmental factors over which they have no control. Or, they choose the negative strategy of turning to addictions in an attempt to create a positive mood.

What if you could automatically switch your mind to a positive state, all without a drink, drug or negative behavior? Would you believe the human brain is capable of that? It is, through a process called "anchoring," and it can make unbelievable changes in your life. The next step is learning what anchors, or triggers, are.

What Is an Anchor?

A good definition of an anchor is a stimulus (behavior) that is associated with a particular mood or state of mind. For example, if you won a substantial amount of money every time you scratched off a lottery ticket, you'd begin to associate scratching the lottery ticket with a positive state. In fact, unintended anchors like that are at the root of many addictions...if the behavior creates a good feeling, you continue the behavior in pursuit of that same feeling.

Anchoring, or associating, is based on the famous research completed by Ivan Pavlov with his hungry dogs. I'm sure you've heard of it. Basically, Pavlov found that dogs could associate the sound of a bell with hunger pains and involuntary salivation. After a training period, Pavlov found that the dogs would begin salivating and having hunger pains at the sound of a bell, regardless of the time that the bell sounded.

You may be asking how that affects us today. What Pavlov found is a term known as classical conditioning. This means that associations can trigger feelings and behaviors without someone making a conscious effort. This is very important in success and how individuals live their lives. Not only can anchors cause problems in your life, but they can also help you improve or change your state of mind based on positive associations.

Here are a few facts about anchors:

1. It doesn't take a long period of time to establish an anchor. You can set a trigger quickly, and repeated motivations and conditioning will reinforce it.
2. Reinforcement and direct rewards are not required for an anchor's association.
3. Internal responses and experiences are significant. Although internal reactions are not measurable, they are a definitive response.
4. Anchors are "set" and "fired." The more profound the experience when the catalyst is set, the stronger the retaliatory response.
5. Timing is crucial while establishing an anchor.
6. The more original the motivation, the stronger the trigger.
7. Anchors can be established in the visual, auditory, and kinesthetic representational systems.

Anchors can be set and fired both consciously and unconsciously. People regularly create anchors in everyday experiences. Say you watch a news show about an incident or situation you feel strongly about, whether that feeling is negative or positive. From that point on, any time a word or image comes up that brings forth the memory of that news show, it will elicit a certain response. In effect, an anchor has been "set" and "fired."

One way to think of it is the old bell curve. As you enter into any emotional experience, the experience will usually start slow and build to a peak, then diminish. If a unique stimulus is applied as you're hitting the peak of the feeling, that stimulus will cause you to enter into that same "state" or emotion any time you encounter it in the future.

Think of the power that holds for addiction treatment. If you could take away the triggers that cause your behavior, and replace them with triggers for positive behaviors, what kind of freedom would that give you?

We've talked about anchors in general, and in a moment we'll look at how they can help you; right now let's delve into the types of anchors.

We all use visual (seeing), auditory (hearing) and kinesthetic (feeling) forms of communication, but we usually have a predominant way we like to think and communicate.

Visual Anchors

Visual anchors are among the most common, because humans are visual creatures. All of us have been making visual associations since childhood. Think about when you were a small child. You couldn't read, but you knew those golden McDonald's arches when you saw them! As an adult, if you drive through a residential area ten miles over the speed limit and catch a glimpse of a white car, what's your immediate response? That's right. You hit the breaks, grit your teeth, and know you're about to be $100 poorer. For someone addicted to cigarettes, even the sight of another person smoking can trigger that nearly irresistible craving.

We make associations every day based on color, appearance, texture and faces. Think about that grouchy neighbor next door; what do you feel when you see his shining face? Now you understand anchoring! The sight of his face puts you in a not-so-positive state of mind, just by mere association.

Not that all anchors are negative. Not at all; there are positive and negative visual anchors. When you see the envelope containing your paycheck, your state of mind turns positive. The sight of a cherished relative brings a positive smile.

You may be a visual person if you:

- Speak quickly (remember a picture is worth a thousand words!), use broken sentences and may jump ahead and finish other people's statements.
- Gesture a lot with your hands and use a lot of pointed movements.
- Breathe shallow and fast; or even get breathless if speaking on a subject you like.
- Are very mindful of how you look—colorful, and like to match (you would rather look good than be comfortable!).
- Look up a lot with your eyes.
- Socialize a lot—you like being seen in the right places at the right time!
- Are a neat freak.
- Are impatient.
- Are result-oriented—get the job done.
- Use SHOW ME as your watch words!
- Think very fast (speed of light versus speed of sound).

- Love graphs, charts, visual presentations, EYE CANDY.
- Like short clear, concise presentations that get to the point.
- Hate being interrupted—you may lose your thoughts.
- Ask questions that stimulate visual responses—"How will this look to the others?"
- Use visual words: *look, see clear, sharp, focus.*

Auditory Anchors

An auditory anchor is a sound that is linked to a state of mind…just like Pavlov's dogs and the bell. Again, it can be a positive or negative state. What do you feel when you hear the alarm clock, Jaws theme or a fire alarm? Most people feel negative, panicked or just plain lousy. That's because there's a negative state associated with that particular sound. When the alarm clock goes off, it means having your feet hit the floor even though you're exhausted. A siren sends panic rushing through your body. "Is someone hurt?" you wonder. "Is it my family? Is my house on fire?"

Those responses are automatic, without any effort from you. If you suffer from alcoholism, the sound of ice tinkling in a glass may spark the compulsion to drink. When you hear your full name in a loud voice, does it summon a bad feeling? I don't know about you, but when I hear "William Danny Horton," alarm bells go off. That's because I've only heard my full name when I've been in deep trouble.

Auditory anchors can also be positive. Think about a romantic movie and the soundtrack that goes along with it. The soundtrack probably stirs feelings of romance or closeness because it's associated with a positive action or behavior in that movie. A song from your youth may make you feel refreshed, energized or nostalgic because it's associated with a positive moment in your own life. This is also the key to working out to "upbeat" music. It can help you get motivated and stay motivated because it inspires an energetic frame of mind. Or, let a former U.S. Marine (there are no ex-Marines!) hear the Marine Corp anthem. Big response!

You may be an auditory person if you:

- Speak slower and are rhythmic.
- Like long conversations.
- Tug at your ears or touch your mouth.
- Have deeper breathing, mid-chest range.
- Are more casual in dress—no bright colors, but still like to match!
- Are slower in your thought process but are more deliberate in your thinking.
- Like to talk things over with others as well as with yourself to check on how they sound.
- Love animals, have a kinship with nature.
- Look to the sides a lot.
- Would rather live in the quite countryside than in a city.
- At a party, will huddle with others to talk.
- Like soothing music at work.
- Are good at handling people.
- Are more open to both sides of an argument.
- May over-explain things!
- Need to be told what to do.
- Need to be listened to.
- Do not like charts and graphs.
- Use a lot of stories and metaphors

- Can be talked out of things by others.
- Use auditory words: *hear, talk, discuss, cry, buzz.*

Kinesthetic Anchors

A kinesthetic anchor is a movement, touch or physical action that triggers a particular state of mind. This can best be explained through the touches, holding or hugging of a loved one. When that special person touches you, it makes you feel special and loved, right? That's because you've associated that touch with the love and affection of that person, which sparks a positive emotional state. On the other hand, what happens when your boss touches you on the shoulder and says, "I need to see you in my office"? You experience an immediate response... *Uh-oh! Am I in trouble?*

Other common examples of kinesthetic anchors are the small gestures or behaviors of sportsmen. Think about a baseball player who beats the bat on the ground before stepping to the plate, or the football player who slaps another on the back end. They do those things because their minds have linked those behaviors to a positive state, usually winning the game.

Now for the big news. It's not only the touch of a loved one or the gesture of a sportsman that can create kinesthetic anchors. You can develop kinesthetic anchors on your own. By creating these anchors, you'll feel more confident, invigorated and ready to succeed.

You may be a kinesthetic person if you:

- Speak very slowly and deliberately.
- Touch your chest or rub your chin, use gestures that draw others in.
- Look down.

- Breathe slow and deep.
- Are very casual in dress, comfort being the key.
- Need to apply feeling to thoughts ("I am not sure how I feel about this").
- Huggy, and may be moody.
- Like parties where you feel comfortable.
- Make a great counselor and brilliant businessperson.
- Like hands-on learning.
- Can read through manipulative presentations and people.
- Do not like graphs or charts.
- May be one step ahead of others in negotiations.
- Use feeling words: *touch, grasp, handle, dig in.*

Using Anchors in Your Life

Anchors are a part of everyday life whether people realize it or not. When you fall in love, you're anchored to the pleasant feeling you get when you're around your loved one. Small tokens such as a love song, beautiful scenery seen on a special date or some other memento from the relationship can trigger this elated feeling that's based on the love we feel for someone else. Anchors aren't set, and there are no guidelines. They're different for everyone.

When I first moved to Florida, I experienced an anchor that recalled long-forgotten memories. I'd go to lunch and would feel somewhat upset afterwards, sort of "down in the dumps." I did what most of us would do; I checked what I was eating and how much coffee I'd had. All was the same as usual.

Then, one day when I went for lunch, the smell of "old lady perfume" was strong. I instantly thought of my mother. She wore way too much perfume, as her sense of smell had been damaged by 40 years of 2 packs of Pall Mall a day. She had died of lung cancer 11 years earlier. The olfactory, or scent, anchor of that perfume triggered old memories and feelings, even when I wasn't aware of it. This is an example of negative anchoring in action! Fortunately, I used my anchoring skills to reprogram the trigger.

Here's another example. A former student shared a story of how he was in a dispute with his wife over one of his daughter's boyfriends. The wife wanted him to tell the boyfriend to get lost. My student decided to defuse the situation, so he put on some music they played at their wedding.

As the songs were playing, she stopped, turned around, and said, "I guess it's OK for her to date this guy." He asked her what brought this on. She replied, "When that music came on, my mind flashed back to our wedding (many years ago) where Mother walked up to me and said, 'I still don't like him.' And you turned out all right." That music fired an anchor installed many years before. But that's not the end of the story.

A few months later, the man took his wife for a weekend getaway on their anniversary. He broke out all the right anchors...flowers, champagne, the works! As soon as they settled in, he put on the same music from their wedding. His wife stopped, grabbed him by the shoulders, stared into his eyes, and said, "Promise me we will not talk about our daughter or her boyfriends." He was blown away! Then he remembered that the last time he played this music, they were involved in an emotional experience. Because this new emotional experience was overlaid on the old anchor, it brought up the last "anchored" experience.

Think about products and advertisements on television, radio and on the Internet. Leading manufacturers like Nike, Reebok and Polo spend millions on positive role models to build positive associations in consumers' minds. Other examples are:

> Coors beer invented light beer years before Miller brought out Miller Lite, but Miller anchored light beer to them. Remember "Tastes Great, Less Filling"?
>
> There were at least five gold rock-n-roll records before Elvis, but who is the King of Rock-n-Roll?
>
> Do you ever hear someone say, "I need to make a Xerox of this?" only to see them make a copy on a different brand copy machine.
>
> When you have to blow your nose, do you grab a tissue…or do you grab a Kleenex?

These are all anchors. The manufacturers may not understand the term "anchoring," but they know it's well worth their money, because consumers make positive associations and simply *must* have the product. This is the reason why there are billions of dollars spent on advertisements every year.

These are great examples of the many ways an anchor can be used—an association, a touch, a sound—to trigger a consistent response. You can use anchors to tap into your memory and imagination and transfer those positive feelings and associations to the present situation.

The good news is, there are key factors when using anchors and, if you can learn how to use them, you'll be able to control your state of mind, just as I did with the perfume trigger. This can set the stage for success in leading a normal, addiction-free life full of energy and a multitude of other positives.

Key 1: Intensity

The intensity of the experience can control how fast the anchor develops the associations. If the experience is extremely intense, the association may be strong after only one occurrence. On the other hand, if the experience is less intense, it may take several tries to associate the state with the experience.

Key 2: Timing

Timing is critical. It's necessary that the correct trigger sets off the desired response. The strength of the response will guide the client's mind in the necessary and desired path. The most effective time for the association of the anchor is at the peak of the experience. As the intensity of the experience lessens, so does the association. If you can maintain this intensity for a longer period of time, you'll be more likely to establish the anchor.

Key 3: Uniqueness

It's best to find an anchor that is unique to the experience. You can use any of the three of the types of anchors—visual, auditory or kinesthetic—independently or all together. The key is to make sure the anchors are used at the same time. Make sure the anchor is something associated with that experience, but not something that is common to other experiences. The result of mixed responses due to a generic trigger could end up being counter-productive. By establishing unique stimuli, you reduce the margin of error and better guarantee the desired response.

Key 4: Replication

Practice makes perfect! Just like anything else, replicating the experience will make the anchor permanent. If you are trying to build an anchor, you may have to exactly replicate it a time or two. If it is an anchor using vision or touch, it needs to be precise to build the anchor in your mind.

Mastering the Anchor

Now, here's an exercise to help you master these skills.

Exercise: Anchoring a Resourceful State

Identify a resourceful state or behavior. Think of something you already do well, some behavior or state you would like to be able to access whenever you choose.

Choose an anchor that is easy for you to remember, that you can use whenever you want to access this feeling. Be sure to pick an anchor that is precise. For this exercise, we'll use placing your thumb and forefinger together as if making the "OK" sign.

Now call up a memory of the behavior or state you would like to have, remembering a time when it was strong. What was it like to be doing that behavior? It is important you see this experience through your own eyes, and not as if you are an observer watching yourself. Take note of what you see and hear and feel as you call up the memory. What colors are around you? Are the colors bright and vivid, or are they soft pastels? Are they clear, or are they slightly hazy and out of focus? What sounds do you hear? Are they soft or loud? Is there singing or talking or birds chirping?

As you imagine this scene, allow yourself to experience being there until the feeling is strong and encompassing you. As you do, touch your thumb and forefinger together as if making the sign for "OK." Hold the position for as long as the feelings remain strong, and when they begin to fade, return your fingers to a relaxed position. Shake your head or move in some way so you can bring yourself back to the present (also called "breaking state").

The OK sign has just become the anchor for those feelings. We don't want to stop there, though. In order to ensure these feelings are associated with that gesture, it is necessary to repeat the exercise a few more times. Each time you do, try to add more details to the memory. This makes it even more powerful. Use all of your senses (seeing, hearing, feeling, smelling, tasting) with the experience, so the connection between the memory and the anchor becomes powerful. It is important to remember anchors should be set at the peak of the experience.

The purpose of setting the anchor is to be able to call up the desired state when needed.

Test the anchor. Think of a different experience and make the OK sign as you do, the same way you did a few minutes ago. (This is known as firing the anchor.) What happened? Did you recall the memory in all its detail, complete with the feeling or state you were trying to recapture? If you didn't, keep trying. Sometimes a little practice is all that is needed. Remember, the sensations in an experience will often rise and fall, so you want to set the anchor as the experience is reaching its peak and remove it when the feeling begins to fade.

Now, anchors aweigh!

Beliefs

The power of belief is the *single most important thing* a human has.

It's no secret that some people are more successful than others. Why is this? Most people think truly amazing or successful individuals were handed all the right cards in life, such as a powerful family, wealth or a great home life. Is this true? Are successful people smarter, are they better businessmen, or do they have something that others lack? If you look at history, you'll see that it's not necessarily any of the above. Rather, it's something in the internal operating system of their brains.

Look at Mahatma Gandhi, Ho Chi Min or the Wright Brothers. None of these folks were extremely powerful or came from great wealth. They were all common individuals, lawyers or bicycle repairmen. Yet they accomplished great things, because they expected nothing less of themselves.

That internal operating system within the brain is the place where individuals determine what they expect from themselves. People always live up to their own expectations. If you expect to fail, guess what? You'll certainly fail. If you expect to be the CEO of a company, you will! It's all in the power of belief.

The human belief system is a very powerful thing. What many don't realize is that they set themselves up for failure without ever saying a word. Your internal feelings and beliefs about yourself can either make you or break you... they truly are that powerful.

This is not to say there won't be bumps along the way, even with a powerful and positive belief system. It would be fantasy to assume success will simply fall in your lap. There will be trials along the way, but these can be turned into positives by learning from mistakes. This means taking less successful ideas and turning them into feedback instead of failure. The formula for success lies in correcting and tweaking the system.

Beliefs: Personal Potential

Breaking free from an addiction like alcohol or drug use isn't an overnight venture. In some cases, it takes months or years to achieve. Tapping into the creative resources within you is sometimes a trial-by-error system. As you grow in your success, you learn about yourself, as well as your limitations and strengths. This takes patience and time…which is what unsuccessful people often lack.

As simple as it may sound, there's a great lesson here. You could assume that, though a system of success sounds great, it will likely not work. Or, you could absorb it into your internal operating system, knowing that it will provide guidance in fulfilling your dreams. It's all in how you look at the opportunity and code it inside that brain of yours.

Believing in yourself is the absolute most important step in any venture you'll ever undertake. When you take on new challenges and tell yourself that you will succeed, you can and will prove yourself right.

The Pygmalion Effect

This theory is not a new one, but it is one that can make your dreams come true. In 1957, a professor by the name of Robert Merton researched how people's perceptions of those around them influenced their own. As a research project, a young teacher was told she would be teaching a group of gifted students. These students actually were not gifted at all. In fact, they fell within the average, but also had behavior problems.

Very soon, the teacher discovered that the students were not engaged, interested or willing to behave under her current teaching style. She worked very hard to come up with a new approach. When she did, she sparked the curiosity of those students. After a very fruitful year, the students were engaged and learning; and they proved it with a 20-30 point IQ jump!

How did this work? Did the teacher turn those average students into gifted students? Yes! She changed her style based on the belief that those students were gifted and that she must improve her teaching style to match their potential. Had she expected less of them, the results would have been very different. Now, can you imagine what would happen in your life if you were operating at the same level of expectation?

Merton's theory developed into what is called the Social Theory, or Social Structure. That's a fitting name, because it's very true. People form their behaviors and expectations around those individuals with whom they're associated. If the expectation is low, then the performance will be also, and vice versa. If you know other people expect you to fail in breaking your addiction, you may form a belief in your own failure. If you have even one person "in your corner," so to speak, you're much more likely to believe in your success.

That's one thing that makes A.A. and similar programs so effective despite their drawbacks. For some people, drinking—or overeating, or smoking—is part of their family background and social structure. They've never experienced life without it. A group program such as N.A. or O.A. may be the only place where they will see people *not using*. Many addicts need a social group where they can see that people can have fun and not use the drug. The need someone "in their corner."

Beliefs and Biochemistry

Your beliefs not only affect your thinking, they also affect your health and wellbeing.

One great illustration of this is the "Placebo Effect." In one study, patients were randomly selected to receive either a "sugar pill" or an analgesic for a headache, without the patient knowing which. Needless to say, the researchers were quite surprised when the sugar pill recipients, believing they received an analgesic, had close to the same results as those who actually received the pain medication!

What does that tell us? It tells us that what people perceive and believe is what happens. The individuals who received the sugar pill believed the medication would work for the headache, so it did. The Placebo Effect is so strong that even the FDA acknowledges the fact that individuals can benefit from a "fake" pill simply because they believe in it. So, do you see how important your belief system is?

Another study did something similar, but they gave one group a stimulant and the other a depressant. The group that was given the stimulant was told that it was a depressant, and vice versa. The results were amazing! The participants reported results consistent with the expected outcome, not the actual medication. Those study members who received the stimulant reported feeling drowsy and groggy. Those who were given the depressant felt full of energy. They actually controlled their biochemical makeup. It was just opposite of the actual effects of the medication, but they told themselves that was how they were supposed to feel, therefore that's how they felt!

Real versus Imagined Experience

Medical science has proven that our brain does not differentiate between what is vividly imagined and what is actually experienced. The same neurological impulses are triggered throughout the nervous system for both situations. This is important for you, because it signifies that, when you close your eyes and imagine yourself succeeding, you are more likely to achieve your goals. In fact, one could say you're preparing yourself for success.

Imagine this to test out this theory:

> *Think of a large yellow lemon...the mere name signifies sour. Now close your eyes and imagine biting into that lemon. The sour juice drenches your tongue, making your nose twitch and your mouth pucker. Feel the cold surface of the lemon on your hands and close to your nose. Smell the citrus scent, reminding you how sour it really tastes. Are you salivating? I bet the answer is YES! That's because your nervous system has been activated just as if you had that lemon in your mouth.*

This power of imagination can work to the benefit or the demise of many people. Some begin to feel fear or stress at the mere sound of a certain situation. This can actually cause them health problems. When the fear response is activated, the immune system can be suppressed, making the individual more prone to illness. How well can an individual function under great stress, fear and illness? How tempting is it to attempt to self-medicate with alcohol, nicotine or food? Fortunately, there's a better way.

Mental Rehearsal – The Secret Weapon

For years, the Russians have dominated the Olympic Games in gymnastics. Many people have wondered, yet never truly understood, why the Russians' performance was so excellent. What's their secret? They employ a sports psychologist. This psychologist offers psychological techniques that enhance the athletes' physical techniques. Not only do the Russians prepare their bodies, but they also prepare their minds.

Think about it...when you rehearse failure in your mind, what are you likely to do? On the other hand, if you follow the example of the Russians and their secret mental preparedness, you can succeed just as they do. When you rehearse the pictures of success in your mind, you soon will be seeing them in person.

Reaching the Mind with Visualization

Visualization is a very important aspect in human behavior. With the power of visualization, you can see yourself in successful positions. You can imagine breaking through the limitations and boundaries that are holding you back. Here is an exercise to help you see the power of visualization:

- Pointing your finger forward, and without moving your feet, turn your body in a clockwise motion as far as you can. Make a mental note of this position.
- Close your eyes and visualize yourself in the above exercise.

- Now, with your eyes closed, continue, but stretch yourself a little further (in your mind). Imagine yourself turning three feet further than you turned the first time.
- Now open your eyes and repeat the first exercise. You went further than the first time, right?

You can get past your mental limits and boundaries that you set for yourself. That's because, when you imagine that you can, you do! Success is just a visualization away!

Breaking Beliefs

Most people strive to reach a record, but never seek to break that record. They never seek a higher goal for themselves. You may be wondering, what does that mean? It means that, if you only strive for something that has already been accomplished, you may never fulfill your full potential.

Take running, for example. Prior to the early 1950's no one had ever run a mile in less than four minutes. After Roger Bannister, a college student, ran the mile in less than four minutes, it wasn't long before others followed his lead. Why was that? It happened because people fail to reach for what they think is unobtainable. Amazingly, after Bannister broke the record, 37 other runners broke the same record that year. What does this tell us? Never take the "top goal" and quit! Strive for more and reach for the unthinkable.

Beliefs Are Never Absolutes

Beliefs are sometimes true, but oftentimes they are only an opinion, a personal perception of a situation. Did you ever stop to think that someone who is feeling depressed would have a different belief about a situation than he or she would when they were feeling better? For instance, if a driver cuts you off on your way home from work, how do you react? If you've had a bad day, you might honk your horn, scream at the other driver, or exhibit other forms of road rage. It might even lead you to go home and grab a can of beer or a bag of chocolate. If you're feeling good about your day, however, you'll probably shrug it off and continue. So, the same event can be perceived quite differently.

People have beliefs about a variety of things they experience everyday, but this doesn't make their beliefs set in stone or rules to live by. Sometimes perceptions are wrong. Perceptions may be off or misguided because of faulty information. Think about the game you played in elementary school—we called it "telephone"—where you whispered a secret in the ear of a person standing next to you. By the end of the line, the details changed. Stories were different, and perceptions were certainly different. See how things can become distorted?

You need to understand that, no matter what the belief, it can change. You need to evaluate each belief and determine whether that belief is true for everyone, or whether it's tainted by some other motive that may inhibit your ability.

The best way to understand whether the belief is positive or negative is to ask yourself whether the belief will hold you back or empower you. Most successful individuals share the belief that all things happen for a reason, and that their lives aren't ruled simply by "fate." The belief that fate or blessing alone provides a successful outcome can cause distress and frustration. Success does not fall in anyone's lap; you have to make it happen!

Beliefs Become True

Saying that beliefs are not always true is simply stating a fact. However, with certain beliefs, the individual often finds that the belief comes true. It has been taught over and over that what individuals believe and think is their fate. We are a product of our internal belief system. No matter how faulty the belief, the person who has the belief will inevitably live it.

People become what they believe because that's how they perceive the opportunity and environment around them. People don't perceive reality, but they do perceive their perception of reality.

Read that sentence again. *People don't perceive reality, but they do perceive their perception of reality.* It's a mind-boggling idea, but one that is unbelievably true. A good example of this theory can be seen when two people have a verbal argument. Both parties are angry. When they think of the argument, they will recall different things. Their minds will take in parts of the altercation, changing, deleting and even distorting the information.

People also have the tendency of remembering a negative expression or action much longer than a positive one. Perhaps a child has done a host of good things, but the one time she messes up, she has trouble living it down. Then, if the child does something wrong again, the parents will automatically bring up the previous negative experience.

People have self-fulfilling prophecies, but not by accident. They set themselves up for such situations. A nagging, suspicious wife can drive even a faithful husband away with her constant negativity. Strong and passionate beliefs can oftentimes become true, because we persist in them until they become reality. If you believe you are destined to be an alcoholic because your father was, or that you will always be overweight because it runs in your mother's family, that's what will happen. So, be careful with your negative beliefs, because you may just create self-fulfilling prophecies that you don't want.

Perceptual Blind Spot

Sometimes the brain will delete something because of a belief system. Have you ever searched high and low for something, all the time telling yourself that you hate looking for things, and that you won't be able to find it because you're so terrible at finding things? Usually, someone else comes along and immediately grabs whatever you were looking for. Often, it was in a place where you'd already looked two or three times. What's going on? Are you having trouble with your eyesight?

No, this phenomenon is known as a *perceptual blind spot.* Because you're so busy telling yourself that you won't find what you're looking for, your eyes scan right across the item without seeing it. This is also called a *negative visual hallucination.*

This idea can be expanded into "blind spots" about success, health, wealth and all other facets of our experience. Beliefs can cause your success or failure in the same way they can cause you to not see a pair of sunglasses or a set of keys. If you believe that there are no opportunities and that you will never be successful, you'll miss the opportunity right under your nose.

The Famous and Intelligent Proven Wrong

Large companies and those seeking advertisements look to those who are famous or intelligent to promote their product. This happens because the public has a positive regard for those individuals, allowing them to believe what they say. But what if they're wrong?

Bill Gates once promoted the fact that no computer needed more than 250 kilobytes of RAM. Dr. Lee De Forest claimed that man would never reach the moon, no matter how many scientific advances came along. In 1905, the head of the U.S. Patent office is believed to have said, "Everything that can be invented has been invented"! So, those who are intelligent, educated, or famous don't always know best.

Never take limitations as whole truths. Always strive for one step better. The four minute mile was once considered impossible. So were cell phones and the Internet! Now imagine living without them. What if no one had ever promoted those new ideas? Our computers wouldn't have the memory or capabilities they now have. No one would have walked on the moon. The four-minute mile wouldn't be run in high schools as it is today. Certainly, our lives would be different without our "needed" cell phones and Internet. (I couldn't even have written this book without the Internet!) Dreams are what make success come true. Dream, and dream big!

Creating Beliefs

Beliefs come from our experiences and from the individuals around us. Beliefs are drawn from friends, family members, educators and local heroes. These perceptions and beliefs are important, because they make us who we are, but we must remember that our beliefs are only as good as our perceptions.

Before the age of 12, you can't protect your subconscious mind. Children will believe things to be true if they're exposed to them. Parents know this on a subconscious level; that's why many parents so closely monitor what their children see and hear. When adults tell children things that end up being true, such as, "The stove is hot," children learn to trust what they see big people do.

What if adults tell us things that become negative beliefs? What if we're hearing big people say things like, "You can't have fun without drinking," or "I can't unwind without a couple of beers"? If a child has a role model who "can't" enjoy a cup of coffee without cigarette, won't that child grow up to believe the same thing? Such negative role models give children the belief that smoking is pleasurable long before they have their first cigarette. That belief makes it hard to give up the addiction. To break the addiction, it's that belief that needs to change.

Even a treatment for addiction can go wrong if it creates a belief that works against you. For instance, remember the disease model? It teaches that abstinence is the only way to deal with an addiction. Many in such programs believe that if they use even a single time, they will relapse and use until they die. Is that a useful belief? No! Living according to that belief, a person who accidentally has one glass of spiked punch at a wedding will relapse and never recover. The fact is, mistakes will be made. Mistakes should be treated as learning tools, though, not as a death sentence.

This leads us to the fact the *beliefs are never absolute truths,* and shouldn't be treated as such. Evaluating your beliefs to ensure that they're not holding you back is of the utmost importance. That's because, as you've seen here, beliefs become embedded into our brains and become our behaviors...which are our lives!

Relapse Prevention

One of the most baffling aspects of addiction is the tendency for an addict to relapse into old habits and behaviors. It may happen after a few days, or months, or even years. Not everyone does relapse. Why do some relapse while others don't? More importantly, how can you prevent yourself from relapsing?

Many people relapse when they're faced with a trauma or crisis. Just because you experience a crisis, though, doesn't mean you need to relapse. To stay addiction-free, one must learn to handle any situation with a new outlook, one where *the addiction is not an option.* Remember, the action of addiction only adds to the problem.

When someone is faced with a trauma or crisis situation, how that person reacts is dependent upon several factors. The first factor is your strategy. Yes, *strategy*. What are your strategies to cope with problems? A crisis is an attack on your private world, on your belief systems. It's vital to fight back. You need to recover the relative normalcy you experienced before the event. You fight back and achieve that normalcy using strategies...steps you take to recover some semblance of control.

Psychology tells us that strategies are learned behaviors, which they are. But once learned, a strategy is put out of your conscious awareness. Even a Pavlovian response can be considered a learned strategy. Think about the classical Pavlov training we talked about in an earlier chapter. A dog is repeatedly presented with food, and a bell is rung. Eventually, the bell alone will elicit a saliva response in the dog. Somewhere in that dog's brain it is learning: Bell = food = eat, or, Food = bell = eat. So it is with humans. We learn a strategy and then we use it over and over, until we replace or change it.

There are a lot of nuances to strategies. There are internal and external cues, as well as the Meta programs we talked about earlier. Everything we do, every decision we make, is based on underlying mental strategies that we develop over time. For instance, how do you decide what to eat when you're at a restaurant? Do you ask yourself mental questions, such as, "I'm trying to drop a few pounds, so what would be the most nutritious food to eat?" You may look at the menu and search your memory for dishes you've enjoyed in the past. Maybe you ask others what they're having. Whichever method you choose, you've developed a mental process, or strategy.

You have a strategy for EVERYTHING you do, and a lot of those strategies overlap. The problems begin to take place when our strategies are no longer working, or when we use an inappropriate strategy.

For instance, you may use the same style of strategy in different contexts. This may or may not be problematic. I worked with a man who used his business strategy (which made him rich) to find a wife. He found his prospect (business venture), did his research (dating), found he wanted to acquire the property, and was willing to pay the asking rate (marriage). So they got married. He then took a hands-off approach, paid the price, and bought the house and cars. Now he was basically ignoring his wife, unless there was a problem (the way he would run a business). What he actually needed was a romantic strategy.

Another example is how you know when it's time to eat. Do you see others eating? At dinnertime, do they feel you must eat? When you see food, is your first response to eat? Or do you feel you must eat when you feel good? What about when you feel bad? If you have a food addiction or weight issue, you probably don't use HUNGER as a cue to eat. A naturally thin person will almost always use HUNGER as the key cue of when to eat. That is that person's strategy. They will not eat if they are not hungry, so they are seldom overweight.

I urge you to track your internal processes when you are making decisions so you can learn about strategies first-hand. This is an advanced NLP process, but once you are comfortable with the idea, it will get easier, and it can be a very useful tool to learn more about how you think and operate in relation to your addiction. Remember the ***why*** is not very useful. If you change the behavior first, you remove the emotional charge. Then you can change the program.

People who have developed good problem-solving skills often find they have formed functional strategies that may help in overcoming a crisis. Unfortunately, a good many people form dysfunctional strategies. One example of a dysfunctional strategy is the formation of *pseudo-solutions,* mental processes that actually hinder your recovery. The psychologist, Paul Watzlawick, coined the phrase pseudo-solutions when referring to a situation where the answer (or pseudo-solution) to the problem is more problematic than the initial dilemma. Such pseudo-solutions are the things that we do, with good intentions, to solve a problem. In the end, though, such a false solution only adds to the level of difficulty.

Here are some common dysfunctional strategies that you may recognize:

Abdicate

When people abdicate control, they become helpless. They look to others for all of their answers. They become passive when faced by a new reality. This is not to be confused with the normal, natural tendency to look to leadership when in the midst of a crisis. This dysfunctional strategy occurs after the crisis has subsided somewhat, yet you still renounce your responsibility for yourself, and want, even expect, others to act for you.

This may also develop into magical thinking, where you expect some "magic" to solve the problem. This could be anything from thinking, "They're not really dead; they will be back," to expecting God, the government or some other entity to erase the problem from history.

We may also try to conform too much. This means wanting everything to be the same, and not allowing any conflicting thought, opinions, or beliefs. Conflicting opinions, we think, may threaten the perceived solution, which is to fit into the new, developing reality.

An aspect that is often overlooked is the tendency to be overly resigned. You may accept everything that happens without putting up an argument, even if you're right and the new circumstance is wrong. You thereby abandon your personal responsibility for decision-making.

When you abdicate responsibility, you may develop a sense of fatalism. Your outlook becomes bleak, embodied by the pervasive thought, "We're all going to die anyway, so why bother?"

Alienate

This is a reaction to the instinctive "fight or flight" response. The solution here, opposite of abdicating, is to become overly controlling. This may show up as aggressive behavior toward a certain group (especially if that group resembles the person or people who caused the crisis). You may also become hostile to all people in general. Another sign of alienation is that you start to exert abnormal control over family members, such as keeping your children from normal activities like going to the mall or football games, due to your idea of a perceived threat.

You also see this behavior in companies that are in economic crisis. A manager will often start to micro-manage every aspect of the business, not allowing workers to do their jobs. Alienation may be the cause of power struggles in both family and business situations.

We also see alienation in the development of a total win-lose attitude, where the person in crisis views everything as a competition. It's also common to see people in crisis start to hoard things such as food or supplies.

Automate

People who automate get stuck in a proverbial rut. You start to refocus your efforts in behaviors that are unproductive, hoping those behaviors will become helpful. This may be seen when you become totally inflexible in your thoughts and actions. You appear (and are) obstinate to others, and become rigid in your routine. During this time, you'll also be resistant to any new idea or procedure.

When you automate, it's not uncommon that the past takes on more value, that the life before the trauma seems idyllic and that people who are now gone are elevated to divine status.

Those in crisis may also start to manipulate others by coercing them into following their dysfunctional behavior. One example of this would be when two family members share a crisis such as a parent's death. One of the siblings accepts the loss and moved forward in her life. She continues to work and interact with her own husband and children. The other sibling moves into a depression, alienating everyone. She then attempts to convince her sister that it is "wrong" for the sister to move forward from this loss. In this case, the manipulation was to elicit a guilt response, but it can also be used for personal gain, such as domination or sexual activity.

Another way automation may manifest is by the person exhibiting excessive individualism…seemingly the opposite of the conformity displayed with abdication. During the time of the Vietnam Conflict, for instance, you would see photos of soldiers exhibiting excessive individualism. They would wear a combat uniform but would have peace signs or marijuana leaves drawn on their helmets. Many photos depicted soldiers wearing jewelry. This was their method of dealing with the crisis.

The most common dysfunctional strategy related to automation is that a person may simply continue to struggle while doing actions that have not worked in the past (which, by the way, is the very definition of insanity!). Although the action has never brought about the desired result before, the person will repeat the unsuccessful behavior without realizing that nothing will change until the strategy changes.

Agitate

A person who uses this strategy will avoid awareness of the reality of the new situation through continued denial. This often leads to drug and alcohol abuse, as the person uses these substances to escape the reality of the situation.

Hyperactivity is a common trait during a crisis. You may attempt to lose yourself in an activity such as continuous housecleaning. You may become a "workaholic," sacrificing 12-16 hours a day to your job in order to escape some personal crisis. For the troubled person, this repetitious, non-thinking movement is a way to shut down the thinking mind and allow a form of automation to occur. In a small way, it also gives you control of a part of your environment, alleviating that helpless feeling. This behavior actually may be helpful shortly after a crisis, but it shouldn't be allowed to continue for too long. At some point, it's necessary to begin to move forward, setting aside these forms of escape.

Naturally, anxiety is prevalent in a crisis. Tension prevents a person from having fun or enjoying life. The crisis—and its aftermath of fear—waits like a coiled serpent in the back of the mind, always ready to pull the person back into its dark coils. This is where depression may start to develop. We're talking about long-term, deep depression. This is often characterized by a lack of participation in normal activities, even to the point where the person refuses to get out of bed. At this stage, there is the impression that the person has no energy or life force. Thoughts and threats of suicide are common.

Secondary Crisis

Once dysfunctional behaviors form, the problem can result in a secondary crisis. This happens when the original dysfunctional strategy develops into a long-term problem.

The most common of the secondary crises are:

Apathy

This comes from the first reaction of passivity, or abdication, but in a longer, more magnified way. You may want to stay in bed or remain isolated. Society can provide strong reinforcement for this behavior. You might hear things like, "Maybe you need some time to yourself," or, "It's okay to isolate." This is caused by overly helpful, protective, or paternalistic people or organizations. They're trying to help, but this response only feeds the apathy, the "why try/why care" attitude. Research has proven that, because humans are interdependent, social creatures, interaction is vital.

One drawback of encouraging apathy is that it may develop the idea that being a victim can be profitable. It may also create a "victim mentality" that will carry forward in all future actions, both at work and at home.

Deep Depression

Deep depression is where one type of crisis (often self-made and reinforced) becomes a cycle of continued crises. This leads a person into deep depression. It can also eventually cause the person to escape into hallucinations, where a true psychosis may develop later, though this is rare.

An example of a self-made crisis cycle would be when the person in crisis feels unable to pay his or her bills, although the money is in the bank. Naturally, this causes another crisis as all bills become overdue, causing the distress of phone calls and past-due notices (another crisis). The next step is the disconnection of the person's utilities due to lack of payment. Each crisis was followed by another, yet the whole thing was initiated by a self-made crisis.

Drug/Alcohol Dependency

It's common to see alcohol and psychotropic drug use increase after a trauma or crisis. Well-meaning doctors can contribute to this by over-prescribing medications. Dependency develops when the usage does not decrease over time. The situation goes from self-medicating into a problem in its own right. Again, society contributes to this problem with the common suggestion, "Have a drink. It will help you calm down."

Relationship Crisis

During and following a crisis, it's not uncommon to see an increase in marital separations due to loss of sexual interest, infidelity or lack of communication. Communication is very important in a crisis. Unfortunately, it's one of the first things to break down. When these personal problems become a pattern, both social relationships and family relationships suffer. Friends pull away or are pushed away. Surprisingly, the loss of a young child is among the most common crises that lead to marital separation.

Suicide/Aggressive Actions

When problems are not dealt with or solved, the end result can be aggression against yourself or others. There is usually an increase in family violence, especially child abuse, after a disaster or traumatic event.

Chronic Psychosomatic Problems

Sometimes initial psychosomatic problems become a habitual pattern. This is not a case of hypochondria, where mental depression is accompanied by imaginary physical ailments. A person with chronic psychosomatic problems is not pretending or imagining their ailments. The condition does require medical and psychological treatment. This happens because stress really can create a "bad back" due to muscle tension. This, in turn, prevents the person from exercising, which then weakens the back. Then, when they do try to lift something heavy, they are injured.

You can see how many problems can be caused simply by the way you deal with a crisis. It's not surprising that, with dysfunctional strategies like these, many people relapse into their addictions. What, though, are functional strategies?

Functional Strategies

The first functional strategy is to survive the event! You then have to learn from the situation and adjust to it in order to develop a plan to live in the new reality. These are the functional strategies:

Accommodate

The primary focus here is on physical and mental survival. Your strength and effort are focused on making sure you and those close to you come out alive.

Next is social survival, where you help those around you, and society as a whole, "dig out" and rebuild.

Then you have spiritual survival. Some turn to faith early in the crisis…it depends on your background and upbringing. It's also not uncommon for people in crisis to question their spiritual or religious beliefs at this time.

Assimilate

These people survive the crisis and accept the new changes in their lifestyle with awareness, analysis, adaptation, and flexibility to their new reality.

Autonomy

When you become active in your own growth through assertiveness, creativity, and accountability, you are using autonomy. This is a functional strategy that follows the pattern: This happened, so...What do I do now? How do I do it? What's next?

Associate

When you associate, you use the crisis or trauma to strengthen family or social bonds. You see families, neighborhoods, and cultures come together through new affiliations, alliances and advocacy. Family and marital relationships can experience new levels of intimacy.

Many of our coping strategies, including those surrounding addictions, are automatic. We don't even realize we're doing them. The great news, though, is that you can use NRT and the power of your mind to change your strategies.

Once you have new strategies, nothing—that's right, NOTHING—can hold you back. There's no turning around. Failure is not an option. You're on your way!

Building Self-Confidence

It's easy to talk about building self-confidence, but how do you do it? Below is a technique you can use to respond to compulsions and stay resourceful, whether it's at home, at work, or with friends...anywhere you might encounter that temptation to return to your addictive behavior. This method enables you to use your urges as feedback to improve your life and your relationships.

Dissociation Technique *[CD1]*

1. See yourself in front of you. That self in front of you is going to learn a new approach to compulsion while you watch from the outside. Do whatever you need to do to feel detached from that self. You can see that self farther away, see it in black-and-white, or place it behind Plexiglas, whatever it takes.

2. Watch and listen as that self experiences a trigger or an urge and instantly dissociates. There are several ways that self can dissociate. Your self can surround itself with

[CD1] I pulled this from the technique in Mind Control that dealt with criticism. I know something of hypnosis, but I'm definitely not a hypnotist, so feel free to change it back if I screwed it up!

a Plexiglas shield when it encounters a certain situation. Or that self can see the words from its past printed within a cartoon balloon like in a comic strip. That self uses one of these methods to keep feeling neutral and resourceful.

3. Watch as that self makes a slide or movie of the trigger. What is causing this craving? Does that self have enough information to make a clear, detailed picture? If the answer is "no," gather information. If the answer is "yes," proceed to the next step.

4. Have that self decide on a response. For example, that self can remain in the situation and choose not to pursue the addictive behavior. Or that self could turn and walk away, saying, "I am clean and sober," or "I am a clean-air breather," or "I see things differently now."

5. Having watched that self go through this entire strategy, do you want this for yourself? If the answer is "no," ask inside how you modify this strategy so it fits you. If the answer is "yes," continue.

6. Thank that self for being a special resource to you in learning this strategy. Now pull that self into you, feeling him or her fill you, so that this knowledge becomes fully integrated into you.

Joe versus the Volcano

In the movie Joe versus the Volcano, there is a scene in which they are out in the middle of the ocean, after the boat has sunk, when they are on the water by themselves. If any of you have been out on the ocean at night, when the moon comes up, it is an interesting experience. It's huge; it's gigantic. In the movie, Joe looks at the moon and remembers his life; he thinks he's going to die from exposure. He stands there and he looks up to the moon and says, "God, whom I do not understand, thank you for my life."

The power of the movie lies in the fact that Joe only has the guts to live when he knows he's going to die. That takes some courage. Joe versus the Volcano is about hope, about reaching beyond yourself. If we realize that we are all mortal, we better begin to think about what is it we want to do. What is your passion, your purpose, your mission?

And what I ask is:

If you can have just a little bit of that kind of gratitude for some of the talents, tools, and abilities you have been given—and you have all these different talents, tools, and abilities—you can really move the world. Sometimes, though, it's hard to take that in and have the "gratitude in your attitude," so to speak. It's difficult just to be thankful for your life.

Breaking an addiction is perhaps one of the least understood sciences in the world. You may think that it's just not possible. I'm here to prove that it is, indeed, very possible. You don't have to be a wizard or a sorcerer, or even a psychologist; all you need to do is read this book till you have mastered all the ideas and techniques described. After all, it's not very difficult, is it? With the tools you'll find in the Apex Program, I know you'll succeed in living the life you desire…completely free of drugs, alcohol, overeating or any other addictive behavior.

Have you ever felt like it was time to close your eyes and take that leap? It can be a very scary thing. I encourage you to spread your wings now and take that leap of faith. What you're about to do just may be the hardest thing you ever have to do. It can be overwhelming. Like Joe, though, it's time for you to start living.

Neuro Linguistic Programming

What if you could break free of your addiction just by doing some simple exercises and trusting that they would work? Would you do them? What if I told you that being able to answer "yes" to that question is the biggest obstacle you'll ever face?

Do you deserve to be happy? Can you have what you want? Do you even know what you want?

Self-limitation is such an intrinsic a part of everyday life that most adults today have long ago written their dreams off as childish and unworthy, or have even forgotten them entirely. Although "life, liberty, and the pursuit of happiness" is written right into the Constitution of the United States, few Americans feel truly entitled to pursue happiness. We work in cubicles on strict, hectic schedules. We're told when to start, when to stop, when to eat, and when to pee. We rush to jobs we hate and then rush home again to chores we don't want to do. We turn to addictive substances and behaviors to help us cope, and then stay stuck in those addictions long after they've made us miserable. We suck it up and stay on the treadmill because we don't believe we have any other choice.

We do have another choice!

We can choose to *discover* who we are and *become* who we are. We can achieve our dreams and then dream even bigger dreams. Far from being a fantasy, this is actually what our brains are designed to do for us. We don't have to wait to win the lottery. We can choose to pursue happiness right now. All it takes is willingness. All we need is an understanding of how the human mind works and how to maximize its potential.

What Are the Risks?

Isn't it risky to pursue an unrealized dream? Conventional wisdom has it that "A bird in the hand is worth two in the bush." Maybe you're not in love with your work, but it pays the bills and you can count on payday to come like clockwork. Maybe you hate what gambling has done to your family, but the thought of not gambling makes you feel panicked and sick. Is it worth it to risk losing something that feels like a sure thing for something that, though much better, might not materialize at all? Psychologists have studied this very question exhaustively. The results are not always what you might expect.

In one famous experiment, people were offered a choice between accepting a guaranteed $3,000 and taking an 80% chance on receiving $4,000. The majority easily chose the $3,000, though eight out of ten times the gamble would have netted them an extra $1,000. It seems that most people consistently choose safety and security over possibility, even when the odds on the bet are very, very good.

Because fear made them focus on safety and security, people who accepted the $3,000 actively anticipated and imagined how much they would regret their choice should they be in the losing 20% of the $4,000 wager. Although they were choosing the security of having $3,000 in hand, they were also choosing to avoid the unpleasant feelings of regret should they wager and lose. A strong emotional component accompanied their financial choice. Fear of loss and fear of regret guided them as strongly as money.

This situation is turned on its head in the case of goal-setting and entrepreneurship. When people feel that they have some control over an outcome through planning, they tend to describe the same risks as...not risks at all! If the $4,000 wager is part of a long-term plan that gives the planner a sense of control over the future, and the hope of a net win over time, the entrepreneur is more likely to take the bet and not consider it all that risky.

People do precisely this every day on Wall Street. They don't feel unduly fearful, because they perceive that they have an investment strategy, a plan that gives them hope that, over the long haul, they will not regret their choices. Sometimes they lose, but they hope to make money. In the long run, they do succeed, because they have a plan. That's one reason 12-step programs like A.A. have always done so well; they don't just tell you to quit drinking, but they also give you a plan.

In other words, to quote risk-research psychologist Lola Lopes, "*Planning is applied hoping.*"

Why should hope overturn fear when it comes to taking risks? As it turns out, the pursuit of happiness is more than just a chunk of rhetoric from Jeffersonian America. Happiness *actually changes how the human mind thinks and reacts.*

Happiness Creates Happiness

The study of happiness has lately become a hot trend in psychology. In terms of the effect of happiness on decision making and risk, though, psychologists have known since the 1980s that happy people actually organize their thoughts differently from unhappy people. Happy people are more likely to see multiple possibilities in any given situation. They are more likely to solve problems creatively than unhappy people. Happy people are better at negotiation than unhappy people, and tend to have more associates and more associations. What is most surprising of all, happy people are more motivated to maintain their happy state than unhappy people are to achieve happiness.

In other words, unhappiness breeds limitation and more unhappiness. Happiness creates possibility and more happiness. Common sense seems to suggest that an unhappy person is in a negative situation and that, if only the unhappy person can make positive external changes, he or she will then be happy. In reality, happiness creates positive changes and seeks to maintain itself as a default state of mind. The unhappy person doesn't need to make positive changes to be happy. Rather, *the unhappy person needs to be happy in order to make positive changes*. Happiness, it turns out, is an inside job.

Let's look at an example. A friend of mine sought the help of a respected therapist because a series of bad relationships had left him in a state of deep and chronic depression. He felt convinced that, if only he could make good relationship choices, he could be happy again. After several visits, the therapist concluded–much to my friend's surprise–that it wasn't the relationships that were making him unhappy; it was his unhappiness that was leading him into bad relationships. After a relatively brief course of therapy directed at improving his internal state of mind, he began to make much better choices. Within a year, he met a lovely woman, whom he eventually married. Today he is happy, and remains so most of the time.

"That's all very interesting," I can hear you muttering. "But how is a person supposed to just get happy? It isn't as though you can pull happiness out of hat."

Well, actually, you can. It's exactly like that. You can pull happiness right out of your hat.

Suggesting Happiness

Sigmund Freud probably isn't the first historical figure that springs to mind when you think of happiness. In his private life and his personal demeanor, he wasn't exactly a barrel of laughs. However, he did popularize a model of the human mind and a method of changing it by which some very unhappy people were made quickly and dramatically happy. Freud discovered that, by inducing a state of deep relaxation in clients and then uncovering a hidden trauma while they were in that deep state, he could cure clients of "hysterical" paralysis. In other words, a woman might come to him complaining of a paralyzed arm, but once the subconscious suggestion was made that her illness was due to an old emotional wound, she would afterward be able to move her arm at will. Freud toured European hospitals showing off this technique (which amazed everyone until it didn't any more).

Freud's technique stopped amazing the scientific community because he thought the curative part of his technique was the release of hidden trauma, which Freud usually construed to be sexual trauma. This scandalized Europe. What's more, it was unclear whether any of the supposed traumas were even real. The fact that the technique actually cured the patients got lost in the outrage over Freud's sexual theories.

Even Freud eventually renounced the technique in favor "talk therapy," or psychoanalysis, in part because he had all of Vienna breathing down his neck over it. What did permanently survive was Freud's model of the human mind as having both conscious and unconscious components. Freud believed that most change happened at a deeply unconscious level of mind, and that the conscious mind, our ordinary waking state, was more like the steering wheel on a car. The unconscious mind steered the car, and the conscious mind went in that direction without even knowing what it was obeying.

Today we know that the part Freud got right was the part about the effectiveness of change triggered at an unconscious level. It's likely that, had Freud skipped the trauma business altogether and simply suggested to his relaxed clients that their paralysis would disappear as good feelings returned, his patients would have had the same positive result. Hypnotists use similar techniques to this day to help clients stop smoking, lose weight and break addictions. Entire branches of therapy have grown up around the observation that inducing deep relaxation and making positive suggestions creates a dramatic shortcut to happiness and changes the way people think and interact with the world.

Clearly, I'm suggesting you get happy. Now what?

Who Is Steering Your Car?

If happiness leads to creativity, increased awareness of possibility, and addiction-free living, and if happiness can be created simply by reprogramming our unconscious minds, why are so many people unhappy? If the unconscious mind is the driver, and the conscious mind is the steering wheel, which is steering your car? If you're unhappy, you're probably not the one behind the wheel. Shouldn't it be you?

Of course it should. How do you get behind that wheel?

People pick up negative conditioning from all sorts of places, but socialization certainly plays a role. Let's take another look at those risk experiments. Psychologist Lola Lopes notes that cultural aesthetics impacts risk-taking as strongly as individual variables. For example, our culture embraces a Puritan ethic of hard work, stoicism, and a general suspicion of pleasure for its own sake.

Because we unconsciously embrace a Puritan aesthetic, we tend to see stick-to-itiveness and nose-to-the-grindstone work for little pleasure as admirable. The Puritan aesthetic is certainly conservative and risk-averse, and it is coded into our unconscious minds in early childhood and throughout our adult lives. It isn't the only way of looking at the world but, to us, because it's unconscious, it feels natural and normal.

Contrast this to a very foreign culture, the Sherpas of Tibet. Sherpas are sheepherders who live on the dangerous slopes of Mount Everest. Sheepherding is their main means of subsistence, but it's incredibly dangerous and risky. Because they must do this work to survive, they have evolved a cultural aesthetic that admires and values risk and daring. The more dangerous a trail is, the more admirable it is when the Sherpa uses it, even when safer routes exist. The locals have even been known to laugh at the trails favored by European adventurers climbing Mount Everest, calling these trails "the Yak trail," even though to us those routes seem extremely dangerous.

The idea that you can choose your unconscious conditioning may seem radical, but it has actually been around for a long time. If you are in a hurry, you can seek out a hypnotist or a Neuro-Linguistic programmer (a therapist who combines what we know about human cognition with what we know about the unconscious), or you can attend any number of motivational workshops. Or, you can start with some of the simple tools in this book and use them at home, at you own pace.

By the way, do you remember my question from the beginning of the chapter? Have you gotten to "yes" yet? It really isn't that difficult to begin, and you have nothing to lose but your own misery.

Relaxation, Visualization, Affirmation

Individual people process information in different ways. Most people lean toward one physical sense more than the others. Visual people will often use language that refers to sight, as in, "I see what you mean." Auditory people might say something like, "I hear what you're saying." People who are very tactile and prefer feeling as a way of knowing the world might show understanding by saying something like, "I think I have a grasp on what you are saying."

Because each person's preferred sense creeps into his or her language, into the actual word choices, NLP therapists learn to identify and manipulate their own language to "model" behavioral changes for these clients. They do this in a variety of ways, the most basic being that they adopt the language of the client's dominant sense: sight, hearing, or feeling. Good salespeople also do this. Effective salespeople subtly mimic the language and gestures of the person to whom they're selling in order to make the sale. This technique is so effective that corporations spend big money on seminars that teach this kind of modeling to their employees and supervisory staffs.

You can use these same techniques on yourself. A recent deluge of motivational books have recently hit the market, touting the effectiveness of deep relaxation (physical sense), visualization (visual sense) and affirmation (auditory sense) as tools ordinary people can use to effect deep changes and achieve goals. They're selling as fast as they're written. They aren't selling out because people get bored and this is the latest New Age fad. They're selling out because the techniques work!

Here are three techniques anyone can learn to break an addiction and achieve happiness:

Relaxation

Learning to relax deeply is a process of getting to know your own body. You can use the following relaxation techniques in the process of reprogramming your mind, but they can also be used to calm yourself when you feel life has become overwhelming...to cope when you feel that compulsion to "use" coming on strong.

A common method called "progressive relaxation" involves becoming aware of different body parts until the entire body is relaxed. Typically, the subject starts by tensing and relaxing the feet, then calves, then the thighs, abdomen, etc. One advantage of this technique is that it also promotes a deep physical awareness that persists even after the relaxed state is achieved.

Deep breathing is another good method of complete relaxation. Practitioners of yoga learn this first, before any postures are attempted. The trick is to breathe from the belly. On the "in" breath, the belly is distended until it is nice and round. Then, on the "out" breath, the belly is pulled in as far as possible. Learning to breathe this way consistently will also result in greater physical awareness after focused practice.

A third technique involves simply sitting quietly and being aware of your breath. This is basic meditation practice. Many variations on meditative techniques exist. Some instruct the student to be aware of the out-breath only. Some involve a "mantra" or personal sound to make on the out-breath, such as the Sanskrit work "aum." Any meditative technique that focuses on the breath will induce deep relaxation and a heightened physical awareness and calm. This heightened awareness continues long after the meditation session ends.

Visualization

Developmentally, the ability to form and recognize images in the mind precedes speech and rational thought. Images work on the unconscious mind by directing conscious attention. Creative visualization is a technique for both discovering and achieving a goal by receiving and/or creating a visual image that then directs the conscious mind toward that object.

Many books have been written on this technique, but a simple method for a beginner is to start with deep relaxation. Once you feel deeply relaxed, if you are seeking the answer to a question, you simply ask the question (internally; you don't have to say it aloud) and wait for an image to come to mind. Take the first image you see, come out of your relaxed state, and write down everything you can about the image in detail. Cut out any pictures or photos you see that approximate the image and post them where you can see them daily. You will find that the image stimulates associations that answer your question.

This receptive technique is good for general questions like, "What do I need right now to be happy?" or "What is the best work for me right now?" Once you have answers to these kinds of questions, you can willfully create images of the life you desire and implant them while deeply relaxed. Imagine your desired goal in as much detail as possible. You, for instance, want to break free of addictive behavior. Imagine yourself living a happy, fulfilling life without the drink, drug or behavior. Imagine what you look like when you are doing this. How do you feel? What do your surroundings look like? How much money do you make?

How happy is your family? What do your surroundings smell like? Imagine this while deeply relaxed. If you like, make a collage or detailed written description of your goal later on.

Because visualization works on the part of the mind that "drives" the conscious mind, these exercises lead you to your goal in a seemingly effortless fashion. Opportunities appear out of nowhere. Happy coincidences abound. Things start to change. It isn't magic so much as *unconscious direction.* In reality, your awareness is expanded by implanting an imagined goal in your unconscious mind, and letting it do the work of getting you there.

Affirmations

In 1920, psychotherapist Emile Coue published a book on auto-suggestion, in which he popularized the now-familiar phrase, "Every day, in every way, I am getting better and better." Though Coue did not use the exact term, his little phrase was in effect an*affirmation.* Since then, affirmations have become useful tools for triggering change. They are used in therapy to change cognitive habits. They are used in motivational workshops to create initiative and drive.

The trick to creating an effective affirmation is to make sure it is positive, and make sure it is in the present tense. For example, "Someday I will no longer be a loser addict," is a truly horrible affirmation. It's negative, and it speaks of a distant future. Much better is something like, "I am a drug-free, attractive person and I love myself." It doesn't matter if you use the drug or behavior every day and hate yourself intensely. Say this every day and you will trigger changes both in the way you look and the way you feel.

Your Responsibility to Be Who You Are

Perhaps, having made it this far into this chapter, you're thinking that this all sounds rather self-indulgent and self-involved...and maybe more than a little bit irrational and uncomfortable. If so, I would ask you one further question:

Who benefits from your misery?

The truth is *no one* benefits. Your family is cheated out of a full, happy relationship with your true self, perhaps even thrown into a situation of dysfunction and abuse. Your employer gets half a performance from you—or less—because you really only want the paycheck to support your habit. You miss so much. You miss not only the things you want and never tried to do but, as the research mentioned here has shown, you literally absorb less of what life has to offer. You notice fewer opportunities than you would if you were happy.

Simply put, you have a responsibility to be who you are, to the fullest extent, every day. Why wait?

Moving Past Regret

Life is full of regret; from the time you broke your favorite toy to the time you broke a loved-one's heart to the time you went on a binge and lost your job, there's always something to regret. It's something everyone faces during the course of a lifetime. It's simply unavoidable.

Moving past regret isn't easy. Many people spend years of their lives and thousands of dollars in counseling, only to end up heartbroken because they don't have the tools or knowledge necessary to move past hurts from the past. Without the understanding or know-how to turn off the "regret switch," individuals become fearful of regret itself, and therefore hold themselves back from life. Eventually, that tactic drains the life right out of them. Even worse, regret can make you turn to a substance or behavior for comfort. Once you take that step, a cycle of regret sucks you in and keeps you trapped in that addiction.

There is hope, though. This chapter will expose the *three levels of regret* and empower you to move past this vicious cycle.

Three Levels of Regret Exposed

Everyone wants to live a fulfilled, successful and regret-free life. After all, that's the American dream. It's impossible to break an addiction, or to succeed financially, physically or emotionally, while staring down the face of regret, but you can change that. Understanding how regret takes hold and why people struggle will help expose the root of regret.

Made to Look Foolish or Proven Wrong

No one wants to be wrong or look like a fool in front of others. It can be as simple as making an innocent mistake or as big as losing a major sale because of being high at work. While this is human nature, it actually holds people back and sets them up for failure. Because they're so intent on being right or not looking bad, they hold back. They settle for less, turn away opportunities and eventually regret their fear. There's often safety in remaining quiet, in not pushing the envelope or taking a chance to succeed, but the end result is that you stay lost in your behavior, buried in the crowd of "average Joes."

TIP: *Admitting failure or a mistake is not easy, but sometimes it is less expensive and agonizing than proving how right you are!*

Could Of – Would Of – Should Of

How many times do people wish they would have invested, sold a stock, bought a home or done something else that could have made them money or led to success? Everyone has something they look back on and utter the famous words, "I wish I would have…"

It's difficult to be successful or happy or sober when we work against ourselves. The fear of making a mistake or doing something that you'll regret conditions you to believe that you're better off not taking a chance. You doubt your good judgment because you fear that, with one small imperfection, you may stray from the all-important "norm." The fear of regret then becomes a ball and chain that leaves you insecure and without the confidence to move forward into a life of freedom.

Bad Associations – the Cause & Affect Strangulation

Humans from every walk of life, educational background and socio-economic class fall prey to this "regret-seeking behavior." For some reason, most people choose to defy all odds because they have a "gut" feeling. They feel they can beat the odds. While this sometimes works, most of the time it lands individuals in hot water and leaves them regretting their actions. Then that "could of, should of, would of" comes out, and they begin playing odds that are even worse.

What makes people do that? Well, the human psyche is a complex structure of information and design that's too lengthy to detail, but it all boils down to one simple phrase: Classical Conditioning. Those are fancy words, but they speak of a very real behavior. Classical Conditioning can be a positive, but it can also be a negative when we use it against ourselves. We're taught from the time we're old enough to talk that following emotions, or that "gut" feeling, will result in a positive outcome. After a while, we build confidence in that "gut" feeling, It eventually gets the best of us.

TIP: *Following a gut feeling is not always a detriment, but when all odds are stacked against the decision the individual should step back and re-evaluate. For example, the addiction rate, gambling odds and many other "statistically" sound decisions are thrown to the wind to follow that feel-good gut feeling!*

Back to Classical Conditioning for a moment: it's human to associate one action or behavior with another. This information isn't always incorrect, but when it's carried over or bleeds into other areas of your life, it can be problematic.

Take, for example, the association between foreigners and terrorists. With the recent terrorist activity, the world is on guard, from the government right down to the lonely old lady sitting on the park bench. Because fear is heightened and people now associate Middle Eastern culture with terrorists, there are tons of false reports.

People walk around in fear. Airports, police departments and other agencies have been observed "profiling," or taking extra precautions with anyone looking like they're of Middle Eastern decent. Is that bad? Well, it certainly could be, because not everyone from the Middle East is a terrorist...not even close! So, the fact—*some* Middle Easterners are terrorists—has become a harmful association, making people believe *all* Middle Easterners are terrorists. See how associations can get people in trouble?

TIP: *If an addict tries a treatment program and relapses, and then fears to try again, he will never break his addiction! One attempt...two attempts...even three attempts don't always signify another failure!*

Taking No Chance Is Safe – Right?

Taking chances is a vital part of life and success, whether it's in one's social life, financial circle, relationships or employment ventures. When we sit and do nothing, it can feel good. It can even give us a little boost, because we didn't hear the word "no" or fail at anything. Regret tells you that if you never admit you have an addiction, and never try to overcome it, you will never *fail* to overcome it.

Unfortunately, while this may be a safe haven for the moment, it can turn into a trap in the future. Years down the road, most people look back at their sedentary—or "lack of doing"—attitude and regret what they have missed. While it's possible that a certain treatment program might not work for you, it is **ALWAYS** a mistake to do nothing! That's because clichés are sometimes true: nothing ventured is nothing gained. By sitting idle, we end up regretting years past. We *still* feel like failures because we didn't take the chance of success or happiness. That's a dangerous place to be!

Regret's Power

Cutting to the chase, it's impossible to maneuver around regret when a person doesn't understand where "regret" gets its power. Where is it fueled, where is it stored, and when is it strongest? While there is no single answer for everyone, there are some very common links to the fuel of regret.

Most people find that they are at the height of regret when they've acted in a manner that isn't their normal or consistent self. When that behavior causes them to fail, be embarrassed or have additional troubles, they find themselves facing the root of regret. This feeling, and the comparisons you make, then set you up for future failure because of your past associations. Let's take a simple example with which everyone can identify.

Example: *You're in a hurry to get home. You normally drive the speed limit and obey the traffic laws, but today is an exception. You intentionally run a red light and end up slamming into another car. All you can say when you get a ticket is, "I never do that, my driving is always responsible."*

Though this example is not a life-altering change or regret factor, you can use it to see how regret is fueled and how it can eat away at a person's psyche. This brings us to our next topic:

Are You a "Doer" or a "No-Doer"?

Most people, at some point in their lives, have been "doers." They take the chance when the opportunity arises and allow themselves to "step out of the box," per say. After a few failures or near failures, they begin pairing the taking of the chance—not the actual problem or cause of the failure—with the negative outcome. This causes them to become sedentary, not taking that opportunity because they fear failure.

It all goes back to the Classical Conditioning that we talked about earlier. Instead of weeding to the root of the cause, they simply begin believing that every chance will result in a negative! Overcoming this conditioning is a journey, but it's a journey you can successfully complete. It's a matter of taking the time to realize that regret is a normal part of life, but that you need to put it in a safe place rather than carry it through life full-time.

Turning yourself from "no-doer" into a "doer" is an educational process of learning how to put things in proper perspective rather than making faulty associations. Becoming a "doer" instead of a "no-doer" is necessary if you ever want to break free of your addiction and live the healthy life you now only dream of.

So, what will you **do** now?

NRT 12 Steps to Recovery

Understand the nature of the problem and accept the addiction as yours and as something you can change.

You have to come to terms with the fact you have this problem, and accept that you are the only one who can do anything about it. This can lead you to also embrace the fact that you can do something about it. The cause or reason for the addiction has nothing to do with the fact that you, and you alone, can alter your fate. Look at your past experiences with the addiction and your path will be easier.

Believe that the solution must come from within; you have your own answers and solutions you can use to reprogram yourself.

"The kingdom of heaven lies within," a great man once said. All the true answers to your problems also come from within. When you develop your own solutions, they are easier to embrace and accept. A man changed against his will remains unchanged. Look inside for the answers. They are there.

Understand and know your personal triggers.

Knowing what sets off your addiction is the first step in stopping a relapse. From the songs that make you thirsty, to the commercials on TV and radio, learn what starts your own compulsions and mental obsessions. Only then can you remove their power over you.

Stop the inner war and integrate the new you.

The deep inner fight against yourself must stop. The part of you that wants to change must overcome and integrate with the part of you that fights change. When the war is over, inner peace is achieved.

Change your thinking by altering your logical levels.

Know where you must change. From altering your playmates and playpens, to developing new friends and beliefs, this is where you design a new life.

Develop new beliefs.

What you believe guides your inner truth. What you believe also has a tendency to become true. If you believe you can, or believe you can't, you're right. Change your beliefs, and you change *you.*

Reinvent yourself.

You have the inner power to design a new you, a you without the addiction or addictive nature. Become the person you want to be.

Develop a spiritual connection.

Find and develop a personal belief in something greater than yourself. All true beliefs are personal. Find and nurture one that can help guide you. There may come a time when you have no defense except your spiritual connection.

Learn to motivate yourself.

When you learn how to motivate yourself to take action, you can achieve anything you want. If you're willing to do the work and pay the price, you can accomplish anything.

Learn a positive mental attitude and self-confidence.

Your inner attitude will become how you see the world. Positive attitude leads to confidence and a better approach to problem solving. People also like to be around those with positive attitudes.

Create a steel resolve.

By completing these steps, you're on your way to developing a steel resolve and iron will.

Armor yourself against relapse by helping others.

The best way to insure your success is to help others on their path to recovery. Share you experiences and your hope. Show them the way.

Research Proving Hypnosis Works for Addictions

Significantly More Methadone Addicts Quit with Hypnosis.

94% Remained Narcotic Free

Significant differences were found on all measures. The experimental group had significantly less discomfort and illicit drug use, and a significantly greater amount of cessation. At six month follow up, 94% of the subjects in the experimental group who had achieved cessation remained narcotic free.

A comparative study of hypnotherapy and psychotherapy in the treatment of methadone addicts. Manganiello, A.J. *American Journal of Clinical Hypnosis* 1984; 26(4): 273-9.

Hypnosis Shows 77 Percent Success Rate for Drug Addiction

Treatment has been used with 18 clients over the last 7 years and has shown a 77 percent success rate for at least a 1-year follow-up. 15 were being seen for alcoholism or alcohol abuse, 2 clients were being seen for cocaine addiction, and 1 client had a marijuana addiction

Intensive Therapy: Utilizing Hypnosis in the Treatment of Substance Abuse Disorders. Potter, Greg. *American Journal of Clinical Hypnosis*, Jul 2004.

Raised Self-Esteem & Serenity. Lowered Impulsivity and Anger

In a research study on Self-hypnosis for relapse prevention training with chronic drug/alcohol users. Participants were 261 veterans admitted to Substance Abuse Residential Rehabilitation Treatment Programs (SARRTPs). Individuals who used repeated self-hypnosis "at least 3 to 5 times a week," at 7-week follow-up, reported the highest levels of self-esteem and serenity, and the least anger/impulsivity, in comparison to the minimal-practice and control groups.

American Journal of Clinical Hypnotherapy (a publication of the American Psychological Association), 2004 Apr; 46(4):281-97.

Hypnosis for Cocaine Addiction Documented Case Study

Hypnosis was successfully used to overcome a $500 (five grams) per day cocaine addiction. The subject was a female in her twenties. After approximately 8 months of addiction, she decided to use hypnosis in an attempt to overcome the addiction itself. Over the next 4 months, she used hypnosis three times a day and at the end of this period, her addiction was broken, and she has been drug free for the past 9 years. Hypnosis was the only intervention, and no support network of any kind was available.

<u>The use of hypnosis in cocaine addiction</u>. Page, R.A. and Handley, G.W. **Ohio State University**, Lima 45804. *American Journal of Clinical Hypnosis,* 1993 Oct; 36(2):120

90.6% Success Rate Using Hypnosis

Of 43 consecutive patients undergoing this treatment protocol, 39 reported remaining abstinent at follow-up (6 months to 3 years post-treatment). This represents a 90.6% success rate using hypnosis.

Freedom from smoking: integrating hypnotic methods and rapid smoking to facilitate smoking cessation. Barber J. University of Washington School of Medicine, Depts. of Anesthesiology and Rehabilitation Medicine. *International Journal of Clinical and Experimental Hypnosis.* 2001 Jul; 49(3):257-66.

90% Success Rate with Hypnosis

Authors report a success rate in smoking abstinence of over 90% with hypnosis. *MMW Fortschr Med.* 2004 May 13; 146(20):16. [Article in German]

87% Reported Abstinence Using Hypnosis

A field study of 93 male and 93 female CMHC outpatients examined the facilitation of smoking cessation by using hypnosis. At 3-mo. follow-up, 86% of the men and 87% of the women reported continued abstinence using hypnosis.

Performance by gender in a stop-smoking program combining hypnosis and aversion. Johnson, D.L. and Karkut, R.T. Adkar Associates, Inc., Bloomington, Indiana. *Psychol Rep.* 1994 Oct; 75(2):851-7.

81% Reported They Had Stopped Smoking

Thirty smokers enrolled in an HMO were referred by their primary physician for treatment. Twenty-one patients returned after an initial consultation and received hypnosis for smoking cessation. At the end of treatment, 81% of those patients reported that they had stopped smoking, and 48% reported abstinence at 12 months post-treatment.

Clinical hypnosis for smoking cessation: preliminary results of a three-session intervention. Elkins, G.R. and Rajab, M.H. Texas A&M University, System Health Science

Center College of Medicine, USA. *Journal of Clinical and Experimental Hypnosis.* 2004 Jan; 52(1):73-81.

Hypnosis Patients Twice As Likely To Quit

Study of 71 smokers showed that after a two-year follow up, patients that quit with hypnosis were twice as likely to still be smoke-free than those who quit on their own.

Guided health imagery for smoking cessation and long-term abstinence. Wynd, C.A. *Journal of Nursing Scholarship,* 2005; 37:3, pages 245-250.

More Effective than Drug Interventions

Group hypnosis, evaluated at a less effective success rate than individualized hypnosis (at 22%). However, still demonstrated here as more effective than drug interventions.

Descriptive outcomes of the American Lung Association of Ohio hypnotherapy smoking cessation program. Ahijevych, K; Yerardi, R and Nedilsky, N. Ohio State University, College of Nursing, Columbus 43210, USA.

Hypnosis Most Effective Says Largest Study Ever:

3 Times Effectiveness of Patch and 15 Times Willpower.

Hypnosis is the most effective way of giving up smoking, according to the largest ever scientific comparison of ways of breaking the habit. A meta-analysis, statistically combining results of more than 600 studies of 72 000 people from America and Europe to compare various methods of quitting. On average – hypnosis was over three times as effective as nicotine replacement methods and 15 times as effective as trying to quit alone.

How One in Five Give Up Smoking. Schmidt, Chockalingam. University of Iowa. *Journal of Applied Psychology*, October 1992. (Also *New Scientist*, October 10, 1992.)

Hypnosis Over 30 Times as Effective for Weight Loss

Investigated the effects of hypnosis in weight loss for 60 females, at least 20% overweight. Treatment included group hypnosis with metaphors for ego- strengthening, decision making and motivation, ideomotor exploration in individual hypnosis, and group hypnosis with maintenance suggestions. Hypnosis was more effective than a control group 17lbs vs. 0.5 lbs on follow-up.

Hypnotherapy in weight loss treatment. Cochrane, Gordon and Friesen, J. *Journal of Consulting and Clinical Psychology*, 1986; 54, 489-492.

2 Years Later Hypnosis Subjects Continued To Lose Significant Weight

109 people completed a behavioral treatment for weight management either with or without the addition of hypnosis. At the end of the 9-week program, both interventions resulted in significant weight reduction. At 8-month and 2-year follow-ups, the hypnosis subjects were found to have continued to lose significant weight, while those in the behavioral-treatment-only group showed little further change.

Journal of Consulting and Clinical Psychology (1985).

Hypnosis Subjects Lost More Weight than 90% of Others and Kept it Off

Researchers analyzed 18 studies comparing a cognitive behavioral therapy, such as relaxation training, guided imagery, self monitoring or goal setting with the same therapy supplemented by hypnosis.

Those who received the hypnosis lost more weight than 90 percent of the non hypnosis, and maintained the weight loss two years after treatment ended.

Hypnosis as an adjunct to cognitive-behavioral psychotherapy for obesity: a meta-analytic reappraisal. Allison D.B. and Faith M.S. University of Connecticut, Storrs. *Journal Consult Clinical Psychologists.* 1996; 64(3):513-516.

Hypnosis More Than Doubled Average Weight Loss

Study of the effect of adding hypnosis to cognitive-behavioral treatments for weight reduction, additional data were obtained from authors of 2 studies. Analyses indicated that the benefits of hypnosis increased substantially over time.

Hypnotic enhancement of cognitive-behavioral weight loss treatments–Another meta-reanalysis. Kirsch, Irving. *Journal of Consulting and Clinical Psychology*, 1996: 64 (3), 517-519.

Hypnosis Showed Significantly Lower Post-Treatment Weights

Two studies compared overweight smoking and non-smoking adult women in a hypnosis-based, weight-loss program. Both achieved significant weight losses and decreases in Body Mass Index. Follow-up study replicated significant weight losses and declines in Body Mass Index. The overt aversion and hypnosis program yielded significantly lower post-treatment weights and a greater average number of pounds lost.

Weight loss for women: studies of smokers and non-smokers using hypnosis and multi-component treatments with and without overt aversion.

Johnson, D.L. *Psychology Reprints.* 1997 Jun; 80(3 Pt 1):931-3.

Hypnotherapy group with stress reduction achieved significantly more weight loss than the other two treatments.

Randomized, controlled, parallel study of two forms of hypnotherapy (directed at stress reduction or energy intake reduction), vs. dietary advice alone in 60 obese patients with obstructive sleep apnea on nasal continuous positive airway pressure treatment.

J. Stradlinga, D. Roberts, A. Wilson and F. Lovelock. Chest Unit, Churchill Hospital, Oxford, OX3 7LJ, UK.

Hypnosis can more than double the effects of traditional weight loss approaches

... An analysis of five weight loss studies reported in the Journal of Consulting and Clinical Psychology in 1996 showed that the " ... weight loss reported in the five studies indicates that hypnosis can more than double the effects" of traditional weight loss approaches.

University of Connecticut. *Journal of Consulting and Clinical Psychology,* 1996 (Vol. 64, No. 3, pgs 517-519).

Weight loss is greater where hypnosis is utilized

Research into cognitive-behavioral weight loss treatments established that weight loss is greater where hypnosis is utilized. It was also established that the benefits of hypnosis increase over time.

Journal of Consulting and Clinical Psychology (1996).

Showed Hypnosis as "An Effective Way to Lose Weight"

A study of 60 females who were at least 20% overweight and not involved in other treatment showed hypnosis is an effective way to lose weight.

Journal of Consulting and Clinical Psychology (1986).

Extra Proof Hypnosis and NLP Works!

Research on Hypnosis for Pain Management

Theory: Research using positron emission tomography (PET) scans, shows that hypnosis might alleviate pain by decreasing the activity of brain areas involved in the experience of suffering. Scientists have found that hypnosis reduced the activity of the anterior cingulate cortex, an area known to be involved in pain, but did not affect the activity of the somatosensory cortex, where the sensations of pain are processed.

Hypnosis Reduces Frequency and Intensity of Migraines

Compared the treatment of migraine by hypnosis and autohypnosis with the treatment of migraine by the drug prochlorperazine (Stemetil).

Results show that the number of attacks and the number who suffered blinding attacks were significantly lower for the group receiving hypnotherapy than for the group receiving prochlorperazine. For the group on hypnotherapy, these 2 measures were significantly lower when on hypnotherapy than when on previous treatment. It is concluded that further trials of hypnotherapy are justified against some other treatment not solely associated with the ingestion of tablets.

Migraine and hypnotherapy. Anderson, J.A.; Basker, M.A. and Dalton, R. *International Journal of Clinical & Experimental Hypnosis* 1975; 23(1): 48-58.

Hypnosis Reduces Pain and Speeds up Recovery from Surgery

Since 1992, we have used hypnosis routinely in more than 1400 patients undergoing surgery. We found that hypnosis used in patients as an adjunct to conscious sedation and local anesthesia was associated with improved intraoperative patient comfort, and with reduced anxiety, pain, intraoperative requirements for anxiolytic and analgesic drugs, optimal surgical conditions and a faster recovery of the patient. We reported our clinical experience and our fundamental research.

Hypnosis and its application in surgery. [Article in French]

Service d'Anesthesie-Reanimation. Faymonville ME, Defechereux T, Joris J, Adant JP, Hamoir E, Meurisse M. Universite de Liege. *Rev Med Liege.* 1998 Jul; 53(7):414-8.

Hypnosis Reduces Pain Intensity

Analysis of the simple-simple main effects, holding both group and condition constant, revealed that application of hypnotic analgesia reduced report of pain intensity significantly more than report of pain unpleasantness.

Differential effects of hypnotic suggestion on multiple dimensions of pain. Dahlgren, L.A.; Kurtz, R.M.; Strube, M.J. and Malone, M.D. *Journal of Pain & Symptom Management.* 1995; 10(6): 464-70.

Hypnosis Reduces Pain of Headaches and Anxiety

The improvement was confirmed by the subjective evaluation data gathered with the use of a questionnaire and by a significant reduction in anxiety scores.

Treatment of chronic tension-type headache with hypnotherapy: a single-blind time controlled study. Melis, P.M.; Rooimans, W.; Spierings, E.L. and Hoogduin, C.A. *Headache* 1991; 31(10): 686-9.

Hypnosis Lowered Post-treatment Pain in Burn Injuries

Patients in the hypnosis group reported less post treatment pain than did patients in the control group. The findings are used to replicate earlier studies of burn pain hypnoanalgesia, explain discrepancies in the literature, and highlight the potential importance of motivation with this population.

Baseline pain as a moderator of hypnotic analgesia for burn injury treatment. Patterson D.R. and Ptacek, J.T. *Journal of Consulting & Clinical Psychology* 1997; 65(1): 60-7.

Hypnosis Lowered Phantom Limb Pain

Hypnotic procedures appear to be a useful adjunct to established strategies for the treatment of phantom limb pain and would repay further, more systematic, investigation. Suggestions are provided as to the factors which should be considered for a more systematic research program.

Treatment of phantom limb pain using hypnotic imagery. Oakley, D.A.; Whitman, L.G. and Halligan, P.W. Department of Psychology, University College, London, UK.

Hypnosis Has a Reliable and Significant Impact on Acute and Chronic Pain

Hypnosis has been demonstrated to reduce analogue pain, and studies on the mechanisms of laboratory pain reduction have provided useful applications to clinical populations. Studies showing central nervous system activity during hypnotic procedures offer preliminary information concerning possible physiological mechanisms of hypnotic analgesia. Randomized controlled studies with clinical populations indicate that hypnosis has a reliable and significant impact on acute procedural pain and chronic pain conditions. Methodological issues of this body of research are discussed, as are methods to better integrate hypnosis into comprehensive pain treatment.

Patterson, D.R. and Jensen, M.P. Department of Rehabilitation Medicine, University of Washington School of Medicine, Seattle 98104. *Psychol Bull,* 2003 July; 129(4):495-521.

Hypnosis is a Powerful Tool in Pain Therapy and is Biological in Addiction to Psychological

Attempting to elucidate cerebral mechanisms behind hypnotic analgesia, we measured regional cerebral blood flow with positron emission tomography in patients with fibromyalgia, during hypnotically-induced analgesia and resting wakefulness. The patients experienced less pain during hypnosis than at rest. The cerebral blood-flow was bilaterally increased in the orbitofrontal and subcallosial cingulate cortices, the right thalamus, and the left inferior parietal cortex, and was decreased bilaterally in the cingulate cortex. The observed blood-flow pattern supports notions of a multifactorial nature of hypnotic analgesia, with an interplay between cortical and subcortical brain dynamics. Copyright 1999 European Federation of Chapters of the International Association for the Study of Pain.

Functional anatomy of hypnotic analgesia: a PET study of patients with fibromyalgia. Wik, G.; Fischer, H; Bragee, B.; Finer, B and Fredrikson, M. Department of Clinical Neurosciences, Karolinska Institute and Hospital, Stockholm, Sweden. *Eur J Pain*, 1999 March; 3(1):7-12.

Hypnosis Useful in Hospital Emergency Rooms

Hypnosis can be a useful adjunct in the emergency department setting. Its efficacy in various clinical applications has been replicated in controlled studies. Application to burns, pain, pediatric procedures, surgery, psychiatric presentations (e.g., coma, somatoform disorder, anxiety, and posttraumatic stress), and obstetric situations (e.g., hyperemesis, labor, and delivery) are described.

The use of hypnosis in emergency medicine. Peebles-Kleiger MJ. *EMCNA* 2000 May; 18(2):327-38, x. Karl Menninger School of Psychiatry and Mental Health Sciences, Menninger Clinic, Topeka, Kansas, USA. peeblemj@ menninger.edu.

In the News...

Hypnosis can help ...a growing body of research supports the ancient practice as an effective tool in the treatment of a variety of problems, from anxiety to chronic pain."

-*Newsweek*, 9/04

"In [hypnosis], you can **attain significant psycho-physiologic changes**."

Dr. Daniel Handel, National Institute of Health

-*New York Times*, 6/02

"Though often denigrated as fakery or wishful thinking, hypnosis has been shown to be a real phenomenon with **a variety of therapeutic uses**…"

-Scientific American 7/01

"…hypnosis is not mind control. It's a naturally occurring state of concentration; It's actually **a means of enhancing your control over both your mind and your body**."

Dr. David Spiegel, Assoc. Chair of Psychiatry
Stanford University School of Medicine,
-Jane Pauley Show 9/04

"Hypnosis has gained credibility in the past five years because of research using the latest brain-imaging technology…. Studies show **hypnosis can help treat a multitude of disorders**..."

-Business Week, 2/04

"Hypnosis can actually **help you lose weight**."

Harvard Medical School psychotherapist Jean Fain
-Oprah Magazine, 8/04

"The technique has been **accepted by the American Medical Association**, the American Psychiatric Association and the American Psychological Association"

Martin Orne, M.D.,
Professor of psychiatry, University of Pennsylvania
-Newsweek, 11/86

"Hypnosis: A **safe and potent** pain reliever"

-Consumer Reports, 1/05

"The purpose of hypnosis as a therapeutic technique is to help you **understand and gain more control** over your behavior, emotions or physical well-being."

-The Mayo Clinic 12/03

"Hypnosis is the **most effective way of giving up smoking**, according to the largest ever scientific comparison of ways of breaking the habit."

-*New Scientist*, 10/92

"On hypnosis...**His total loss, 35 pounds**."

Losing It! The Ultimate Diet Challenge

-*Dateline NBC* 1/04

"... hypnosis often is used to modify behavior and overcome phobias and bad habits – it can help you **make changes that you've been unable to make otherwise**."

-National Women's Health Resource Center 11/03

"With weight loss the evidence is conclusive...hypnosis **does help people reduce**."

-*Smithsonian Magazine*, 3/99

"I should have done it years ago...It's amazing **I didn't even want cigarettes any more**."

Matt Damon describing his hypnosis experience to Jay Leno,

-*The Tonight Show*, 12/04

"...throughout the medical mainstream, it's **common to be used for addiction**...and psychotherapy."

-Diane Sawyer,

Good Morning America, 6/02

"...today it's considered **a respected therapeutic tool**, a well-established method of reaching the subconscious mind. Many patients have tried it and successfully cut back on smoking or overeating..."

-Connie Chung,
Eye-to-Eye, 12/94

"Hypnosis seems **helpful in treating addictions**, and the depression and anxiety associated with them..."

-*Psychology Today*, 9/96

"Want to lose weight? Kick a bad habit? Well you might want to try hypnosis! ... no longer regarded as mere hocus-pocus, it's been shown as **an effective means of helping people** quit smoking, shed pounds, reduce stress, and end phobias."

-*Jane Pauley Show*, 9/04

"Approved as a valid treatment by the American Medical Association in 1958, hypnotism has become **increasingly accepted by the medical community**. Its use for chronic pain was approved in 1996 by the National Institutes of Health."

-*The Capital* (Annapolis, MD), 4/04

"There's entrancing news about hypnosis; it's gaining credibility as a treatment for **a multitude of troubles**, from nicotine addiction to post-traumatic stress disorder."

-*Business Week*, Feb 2/04

"It is employed today to **combat phobias, control bad habits** and **enhance performance**."

-*Smithsonian Magazine*, 3/99

"Can Hypnosis Help You Lose Weight? **I'm 32 Pounds Lighter**."

Ira Allen, Center for the Advancement of Health
-*Washingtonian*, 3/02

"...hypnosis can help adult patients control other forms of pain, relieve gastrointestinal problems, **stimulate weight loss**, clear up skin problems, and accelerate the healing of bone fractures and surgical wounds."

-*Consumer Reports*, 1/04

For Contact and Help

William D. Horton Psy.D. CAC
www.drwillhorton.com
941-468-8551